An Introduction to
Disability Studies

David Fulton Publishers
London

David Fulton Publishers Ltd
Ormond House, 26–27 Boswell Street, London WC1N 3JD

First published in Great Britain by David Fulton Publishers 1998

Note: The right of David Johnstone to be identified as the author of this work has been asserted by him in accordance with the Copyright, Designs and Patents Act 1988.

British Library Cataloguing in Publication Data
A catalogue record for this book is available from the British Library

ISBN 1–85346–493–7

Typeset by Kate Williams, London
Printed in Great Britain by The Cromwell Press Ltd,

Contents

Introduction

The study of disability as an academic subject is of relatively recent origin. However, for a number of years disability and disabled people have helped to support an industry of caring professionals, who have sustained the perception of disablement as a 'problem', an individualising and distinguishing marker of difference. The force of the disability movement has begun to raise a collective consciousness of the lack of rights that disabled people have. Legislative change in the form of the Disability Discrimination Act 1995 in the United Kingdom and the Americans with Disabilities Act in the USA has been one method of responding to these inequalities. Any study of people at the margins tends to suggest a sociological bias to the discipline and such is the case with Disability Studies. However, the study of disability crosses academic boundaries and draws on a variety of disciplines, including philosophy, sociology, psychology and history, in order to analyse issues concerning the relationship between disability, social justice and political understanding.

Classical Greek theatre is effectively both the historical and the cultural starting point for linking the image of impairment with judgements about social acceptability. Hevey (1992) and Barnes (1994) have developed the analysis and evaluation of the negative image of disablement and the threat to quality of life that disability historically carried with it for the non-disabled majority in the community. Images of disabled people have become part of both children's literature and adult horror magazines and videos. All of these representations are readily available in every home. They have tended to continue to portray a contradictory image of disabled people:

> They are either pathetic victims, arch villains or heroes. The stereotype of the disabled child is either that of the brave little lost boy/girl overcoming personal tragedy, or of the scheming malcontent determined to have revenge on society for the misfortune that has befallen him/her. (Johnstone 1995, pp. 4–5).

Probably the most common stereotype is the image of the disabled person as pitiable and/or pathetic. This has been used to advantage by charities for the annual TV shows *Children in Need* and *Telethon*. It is interesting to note how this sentimental depiction of disabled people to a non-disabled world has shifted towards the encouragement of a more critical reflection on disability issues; the self-help projects and attempts to inform the public in the appeals of Comic Relief are a good example.

However, Disability Studies is not so much about identifying characteristics of sensory or physical loss; nor about learning facts, although there are some to be addressed and remembered. It is not even, solely, concerned with the circumstances of disabled people. Disability Studies is more about the development of critical enquiry into those social and political forces that frame and inform our relationships with each other and the institutions of society that we have created. As with any study of human encounters there are ambiguities and inconsistencies that must be taken into account when deciding what disablement actually means. These can be multiplied by the additional complexities imposed by any apparent deviations from what is generally considered to be the norm. However, there is no single accepted consensus for what is 'normal' and there are relatively few definite statements of agreement that can be made in relation to the construction of disability. This applies to disability either as an individual label or, more collectively, as an area of academic enquiry.

Whilst this text sets out to describe Disability Studies as essentially an academic discipline, it would be impossible to ignore the private experiences of loss, pain, discomfort and chronic illness that are associated with the experiences of disabled people and their sense of marginalisation. These personal circumstances contrast with the more public, collective experience of disability as a political movement and thereby a more orthodox arena for academic debate and analysis.

Thus, disability is often both subjectively experienced and objectively defined as if it were a problem by both disabled and non-disabled people alike. Coleridge (1993) has indicated how the powerful negative images of disability help to perpetuate a range of emotions including fear, pity, or admiration, depending on how a person appears to be 'coping':

> Much of the apparent confusion and contradictions about disability issues can be resolved through the realisation that disability provides, for the disabled person, a certain experience or set of experiences that are not shared by other people. These experiences do set disabled people apart, but they also bind them, as it were, closer to life itself and its purpose. (Coleridge 1993, p. 215)

Disability Studies has emerged as a discipline for academic study in universities over the course of the last decade. It has grown in schools and colleges; with no official place in the National Curriculum, it has nevertheless shown itself to be an area of concern, driven by interest in both the place and the rights of disabled people. Above all it has emerged as disabled people themselves have begun to question society's definition of them as odd and abnormal or so-called cripples (Driedger 1989).

The book sets out to explore in a straightforward manner some of the key themes that link Disability Studies with wider explorations of equal opportunities and social justice. In Chapter 1 the philosophical and historical background that forms the backdrop to the differing explanatory models of disability are described. There are clearly layered hierarchies of discourse that emerge from these explanations as there are in all spheres of the social sciences. Disability Studies, in searching for a satisfactory language of explanation that challenges preconceptions of dependency and care, shares a dilemma in common with the discourses around special needs and inclusive education. Chapter 2 attempts to develop this issue by examining some of the ideological prejudices that continue to oppress disabled people together with the role that the organisation of educational opportunities and employment plays in structuring the boundaries of achievement that are imposed on the lives of many disabled individuals. Thus the correlation between disability and ageing is questioned as are the attempts to construct care in the community. Chapter 3 is a comparison between the emerging legislation around disability discrimination legislation in the USA and the UK. At the heart of Chapter 4, which sets out to examine the issue of quality of life, there is an appraisal of rehabilitation programmes and an evaluation of the tension between subjective and objective indicators of both satisfaction and dissatisfaction. It is well known that disabled people experience limited choices and this isolation of their experiences serves to highlight the inequity of disablement. In emerging economies, or those societies recovering from civil conflicts, quality of life is measured on a different scale from the considerations being pursued in more settled and established communities.

It is in Chapter 5 that the ethical issues of the right to life are addressed. The historical legacy of eugenics that has been associated particularly with people with learning difficulties and this is traced through to the current concerns over genetic engineering in relation to people with disabilities. Chapter 6 explores the development of the politicisation of disability and its link to the concept of citizenship. The growth of the disability movement in the UK is traced through from its beginnings to its current position.

Chapter 7 sets out some of the considerations for participative research in relation to the study of and with disabled people. The ethical considerations of disabled people as research participants rather than research subjects are examined. In Chapter 8 the impact of some health risks from birth to adulthood are explored, as are some of *Health of the Nation* initiatives, for people with disabling conditions. The effects of dietary controls in relation to people with specific learning difficulties, e.g. hyperactivity, absenteeism caused by obesity-related illness, are also examined and discussed. Strategies for developing leisure and sport activities for disabled people and the effects on levels of fitness are also explored. Chapter 9 reflects on some of the architectural and wider environmental considerations, including access to communication aids, which offer opportunities to remove the sense of marginalisation and isolation felt by many disabled people and thus promote the development of a more inclusive society. Finally Chapter 10 reflects on the future direction that Disability Studies may take as an academic discipline, as we enter the twenty-first century.

CHAPTER 1

Why study disability?
Some explanatory beginnings

Questions

- What are the competing explanations for the oppression and 'invisibility' of disabled people?
- What do you think might be wrong with a social model of disablement?
- What do you consider to be some of the fundamental controversies and challenges posed by the study of disability?
- Is an academic study of disability only possible in advanced capitalist economies?

Introduction

The study and explanation of disability as difference is not new; disablement has been a distinguishing feature marking individuals throughout the centuries. Disability Studies, on the other hand, is a relatively recent area of academic study with, as has been said, a tendency to cross disciplinary boundaries.

The conceptual underpinnings of Disability Studies as a discipline have therefore tended to borrow vocabulary, and thereby definitions, from other areas of the social sciences. As a consequence, discourses around disablement have been dominated by association with the language of medicine, psychology and sociology. The distinctions between impairment, handicap and disability developed by the World Health Organisation (WHO) have remained a universal benchmark for any documentation on 'disability'. The three terms have, deliberately or not, emphasised the layers of discrimination that link disablement with both medical interventions and individual tragedy as economic loss. They form a hierarchy of oppression which, in turn, has been judged as inadequate. This has been highlighted and emphasised in the bizarre and frequently undignified attempts by life insurance companies to justify a value-distinction on bodily loss as a result of an accident or injury, e.g. is the loss of four fingers and a thumb more or less financially traumatic than the loss of speech? The WHO categories also emphasise the sheer number of medically determined disabled people that there are in the world. The first estimates of the incidence of disability conducted in the 1970s suggested that 10 per cent of any population was likely to be disabled (World Health Organisation 1982). This estimate included disability associated with malnutrition; when this is excluded the figure is between 6 per cent and 7 per cent of the human population, equating to a global figure of 245 million disabled, impaired and handicapped people worldwide (Helander 1993).

The International Classification of Impairments, Disabilities and Handicaps (ICIDH) (Wood 1980) developed by the World Health Organisation tended to inform the discourse as a starting point for causality rather than offering any analysis. Over the intervening years these definitions have been scrutinised and rejected, most noticeably by disabled people and their organisations. The assumptions that underpin the terminologies have been criticised for the way in which they perpetuate images of negativity and disability as disadvantage.

Labelling and stereotypes

There is some controversy over terminology in relation to the category or label 'disabled'; however, it would be difficult to believe that being labelled 'disabled' has no effect on a person's feelings about him or herself. Preconceptions about how individuals with disabilities are expected to act are held by many people and it is often believed that certain kinds of social behaviour are an inevitable consequence of the disabling condition.

Labelling has long been associated with disablement and the history of the disability movement is littered with descriptions taken from the school playground, the workplace, religious texts and superstitions. The labels themselves have emerged from the implicit disapproval and associations with 'unworthiness' that lie at the heart of society's judgement of normative differences and disability as deviance. Deviance in this context is considered as behaviour that is interpreted as being abnormal and thus unacceptable by the dominant cultural group in society. Formal and informal law individualises deviance through labelling. Rather than transcending acts of discrimination by appearing impartial and neutral, the officers of law and the judiciary are subject to the same prejudices as those from whom they are meant to stand apart.

Lack of shared meanings about the value attached to disability versus ability means that it is possible to portray people as stereotypical economic units of production. The image of disabled people as 'crippled' or broken units of industrial production fits well with the historical legacy of the almshouse, the industrial revolution and the asylums. It also reinforces the historical characterisation of disability as solely a functional condition or as a personal deficit. The perception of disability as biologically determined reappears throughout history. It runs alongside the ancient, antagonistic associations between good and evil. The evil, demonic and frequently masculine forces that lead to impairment, disability and handicap are pitted against the gentler, more feminine and regenerative sources of goodness. The principal features can be outlined as follows:

- Males are stereotyped as units of industrial production: females are stereotyped as units of service and reproduction.
- The stereotypical image of the disabled person reinforces the image of 'crippled' production.
- The emergence of 'need' builds on the more feminine stereotype of the servant/carer.
- Diversification of people's performance as economic units in a post-industrial society brings the search for alternative roles.
- The structure and definition of disability shifts to include role diversification and disabled people become both a source for newly feminised professional services and service providers.

Stigma and disability

Labelling, or diagnosing the physiological or psychological state of a person, has long been important as a means of determining individual pathology or functional disability. It not only serves as a basis for undertaking curative or remedial treatments but is also clearly linked to medical-biological diagnosis and individual treatment.

Labels may emerge as a consequence of embarrassment, shame or stigmatisation. One of the inherent evils of labelling is that the label comes to be viewed as an attribute of the individual concerned. A learning difficulty, for example, may be associated with a disease within an individual. This contrasts with the view that learning difficulties arise as a consequence of the relationship of variables within an individual's social environment. Put simply, behaviours that constitute abnormality or emotional disturbance in one group in society may not be considered as such in another society or social situation.

There are, of course, a number of arguments in support of the benefits of labels.

- It is often noted that funding and administrative decision-making is based on labels and therefore labelling is necessary in order to acquire funds.
- Labelling a population helps professional carers, researchers and service providers to communicate to one another about what kinds of impairments and disabilities are being referred to (e.g. in evaluating research studies it is helpful to know the characteristics of the population with whom the investigation was carried out).
- If the present labels were to be abolished a new set of labels and/or descriptive terms would evolve to take their place. In other words people with disabilities will probably always be perceived as being different. (However, people do not necessarily need a label in order to recognise that there are individual differences in behaviour.)
- Labelling helps to spotlight issues and causes for the general public. Charities, for example, have relied on taxpayers reacting sympathetically to the characteristic stereotype of a group of people or a cause that has been labelled in accessible language.

Stigma as an extreme form of labelling has come to be associated with some of the more negative features of definition. Goffman, one of the main authorities to discuss the term, sees its origination in the ancient Greek culture that associated stigma with 'bodily signs designed to expose something unusual and bad about the moral status of the signifier. The signs were cut or burned into the body and advertised the bearer was a slave, a criminal or a traitor' (Goffman 1970, p. 21). Stigma has, thus, become a term usually identified with a variety of socially inferior attributes that in their turn are assumed to be associated with a group or an individual. The term concerns deviance from a supposed norm and tends to be ascribed as a permanent attribute. As an aside, this may help to explain why trainspotters tend to be considered merely eccentric, whereas disabled people are stigmatised as a group.

Critics of Goffman's view have suggested that this stance supports a normative view of the unchanging nature of society, e.g. Finkelstein (1979) has accused Goffman of neutralising the insidious role that stigma plays in justifying the maintenance of oppressive relationships between different social groups. Thus, stigma buttresses and maintains a status quo in a system where one stratum of society can continue to oppress another. If this perspective is applied to disabled people it begins to suggest that disabled people are responsible for their own suffering and that the rest of society is somehow relieved from any responsibility for its remediation. In such circumstances it is easy to see how the stigmatised are expected to seek out a role for themselves that is tantamount to acceptance and passivity. This also continues to maintain a view of themselves that is dependent and segregated.

Stigma, as an extreme form of labelling, tends to be associated with victimisation of individuals or groups. The relationship between stigma, disablement and labelling theory is closely allied to the problem of prejudice:

> Disability is the product of definitions and practices that seek to exclude individuals who might be seen to deviate from the socially constructed norms of the 'able bodied'. In short, 'disability' is what a 'disablist' society decides so to call . . . . It is not the inherent nature of disability that matters, but the labelling process, which categorises people by virtue of their position in relation to the dominant structures and values of the society. (Bury 1996, p. 25)

The evidence from labelling and stigma-theory suggests that expectations concerning disabled people can be biased by stereotypes. For example Szivos (1992) reminds us that when we write and speak of 'people with learning disabilities' we are unconsciously condoning the devaluation of one of their defining attributes as a collective group. By relegating some disabilities to the status 'of an almost unmentionable afterthought' some of the positive assertions attributed to other minorities are ignored, e.g. the proud assertions of the gay pride movement and sisterhood are denied to people with disabilities:

> Would we now use the apologetic phrasing of 'people who are black' or 'people who are female' when we have the proud assertions 'black people', 'women' or 'sisters'? I think not. Perhaps it is too soon to envisage a similar slogan of 'slow is beautiful'. (Szivos 1992, p. 127)

Impairment, disability and handicap

The search for an agreed model and definition of disability has been most eloquently explored and explained in the United Kingdom by Oliver (1990, 1996a, 1996b). Much of the writing in the 1970s and 1980s attempted to explain the dominant relationship between illness, impairments and disablement.

The legal definition of disability in the United Kingdom is set out by the Disability Discrimination Act 1995. It is a masterpiece of ambiguity. The definition draws on terms which are themselves fraught with complexity in their interpretation:

> A person has a disability if he has a physical or mental impairment which has a substantial long term adverse effect on his ability to carry out normal day to day activities. (Disability Discrimination Act 1995, p. 1, HMSO 1996)

The experience of disablement is immediately grounded in the association of disability with individual loss of function, rather than with any collective act of discrimination by society. As a result the understanding of impairment or loss as the legitimate basis for disability is reinforced.

This definition acknowledges and reinforces the link with chronic illness as the foundation for the disadvantages that disabled people experience. The causality of disability is explained hierarchically and in the context of personal health. This is consistent with the following classifications devised by the World Health Organisation (WHO 1976, International Classification Document, A29/INF.DOC/1):

> *Impairment* – In the context of health experience, an impairment is any loss or abnormality of psychological, physiological or anatomical structure or function

(i.e. it emphasises any medical damage, or malfunction of a part of the body, such as a stutter, a loss of vision).

> *Disability* – In the context of health experience, a disability is any restriction or lack (resulting from an impairment) of ability to perform an activity in the manner or within the range considered normal for a human being

(i.e. disability is considered to be an effect on bodily functions arising from an impairment. As an illustration, one of the consequences of a stutter might be conversational difficulties, or mobility difficulties arising from spina bifida).

> *Handicap* – In the context of health experience, a handicap is a disadvantage for a given individual, resulting from an impairment or a disability, that limits or prevents the fulfilment of a role that is normal (depending on age, sex, social and cultural factors) for that individual

(i.e. the handicap arises as an effect or consequence of disability in an individual's social setting or day-to-day environment. This might be illustrated by the lack of access to a mobility aid, or a pair of spectacles).

The construct of 'disability' is seen here to be a function of those practices and perceptions linked to certain bodily, mental or behavioural states. The associations with disability as illness are clear. The cultural, social and environmental variables that have come to be the defining characteristics of the social model of disability are more evident in the original WHO definition of handicap. The general acceptance of the term 'disabled' in place of the label 'handicapped' has been one of the significant factors to emerge during the last decade as attempts have been made to harmonise the concepts. In order for this to occur the language of definition has had to change. So too have perceptions of disability and disabled people. Theories of 'social oppression' and the emergence of the disability movement have increasingly challenged attitudes to discrimination and the exclusionary language employed to describe practices.

The need to reconstruct the language of disability

All academic disciplines create their own imagery and language. Disability Studies is no exception. However, the historical legacy of disability as personal tragedy means that there is a close association between disability and personal or biological loss. This has locked the study of disablement and its consequences into a hierarchy of terminologies and oppressive metaphors. For example, the dominant paradigms of care and need have been built around medical conditions and playground name-calling. As a relatively new area of discourse, Disability Studies borrows terminology and definitions from the language of older and more dominant disciplines, such as medicine, psychology and education. But there are dangers that the content of Disability Studies may become reduced, rather like the study of 'special need' in education which is more reflective of a professional ownership in both the definition of the condition and its remedy.

The most difficult level of discourse to counteract in Disability Studies is the ideological. The ideological language of 'ownership' is usually embodied in practices thought to be acceptable and 'normal' and the practices that emerge are, therefore, never considered to be discriminatory. Professional practices with and about disabled people are often perceived in this way since they have developed within an individualistic ideology that makes the disabled person believe that they must take full responsibility for their difficulties. Things are undertaken and done to disabled people for their own good, e.g. specialist categorical services, segregation in day centres or group homes. Perhaps the most insidious aspect of these dominating ideologies is that although the solutions are individualistic, they, in fact, serve to further devalue individual differences and re-emphasise certain 'normal' images of people.

Corbett (1996) has usefully identified how patterns of special language discourses have created and shaped the structure and formal process for meeting the needs of marginalised groups. Just as with the emergence of the language of special education, the dominant discourses of Disability Studies have tended to be set down in a layered hierarchy. The formal terminologies noted by Corbett have shaped the legislative and curricular changes in the framework of special education. They have also played a dominant role in the shaping of Disability Studies as a critical discipline:

The languages hierarchy of disability

medical

psychological

sociological

philosophical

political

educational needs

civil rights

disability arts

These status-rich disciplines, replete with their own terminologies, sit somewhat uncomfortably on top of each other, forming a subtext to Disability Studies. It is unlikely, for example, that the discourses that perpetuate the medical model of disability are going to be greatly disturbed or influenced by the emerging idioms of the disability arts. The voices of the disability arts, in their turn, are different from the discourses centred around political activism 'where new languages and metaphors are emerging in a creative burst of pride and assertion' (Corbett 1996, p. 33) amongst disabled people.

Extending Corbett's argument, Disability Studies appears to offer an opportunity to break away from the confinement of a disablist vocabulary. The cross-fertilisation of ideas from a range of disciplines in Disability Studies provides an arena that enriches and challenges the way in which we can use language. It also highlights the spirit of inclusiveness that lies at its heart. Thus, what Disability Studies offers is an opportunity to create a new model with different explanatory power. Instead of the vertical hierarchy of power illuminated above, there are possibilities for creating a more collaborative and inclusive discourse.

The construction of an inclusive language

feminism/sexuality

race/gender/culture

politics/subcultures

disability/arts/culture/music

parents/radical professionals

disabled people

children with special needs

In the language of this model no single voice is allowed to dominate the emerging discourse. The notions of disability as loss and restriction are removed. Instead they are replaced by the language of inclusiveness, through contact with a diverse range of related and relevant participants. This creates new alliances and shared experiences. The hierarchy of oppressions and marginalisation is replaced by echoes of the 'rainbow coalition' which brought together the variety of marginalised constituencies that fought for civil rights in the USA in the 1980s.

The beginning of disability pride

In 1976, the first seriously political coalition of disabled people was created in the United Kingdom. The Union of the Physically Impaired Against Segregation (UPIAS) published a monograph 'Fundamental Principles of Disability', in which disabled people gave their definitions of disability, based on their lived experience (Finkelstein 1993). These definitions only served to emphasise the limitations and confusions of the WHO classification. The UPIAS argued that medical professionals and other 'experts' were confusing both the language of definition and the contrast between physical impairment and disability. Moreover, the UPIAS argued, people with physical impairments became disabled because they were isolated in institutions, or otherwise prevented from a full participation in social and economic life, e.g. by inadequate access, or by exclusion from the labour market. Thus, to the UPIAS a physical disability was interpreted as a form of environmental and social oppression, rather than a range of limitations arising from a medical condition. Instead of the causal connection identified in the 1976 WHO classification, the UPIAS set out to deliberately differentiate and politicise the two conditions of a disability and an impairment:

> *Impairment* – emphasising the lack of all or part of a limb; or having a defective limb, organ or body mechanism. In other words it tends to emphasise the individual.
> *Disability* – emphasising the disadvantage or restriction of activity caused by a contemporary social organisation which takes no or little account of people who have physical impairments and thus excluding them from the mainstream of social activities.
>
> (UPIAS 1976, p. 14)

Some six years later Disabled People's International (DPI), developing their own causal definitions from the earlier UPIAS construction, moved the focus of causality even more to the impositions and barriers erected by society on people with impairments. By building comparisons with what might be considered 'normal life' and the restrictions placed upon people with impairments and disabilities, the DPI placed causality within the schema of community living:

> *Impairment* – the functional limitation within the individual caused by physical, mental, or sensory impairment
> *Disability* – is the loss or limitation of opportunities to take part in the normal life of the community on an equal level with others due to physical and social barriers.

> (DPI 1982)

Thus, the focus of definition had shifted along a continuum of normality within the course of ten years. Within what Oliver (1996b) has described as 'the politics of difference', the UPIAS model demonstrates the more radical end of this continuum. It suggests the beginning of a conscious disability pride, a disability culture and, moreover, the restrictive boundaries of notions of normality.

However, the WHO conceptions of disability have tended to be established by non-disabled people speaking on behalf of and about disabled people. The DPI definition has caused a change of consciousness and a shift in awareness away from the pathology residing within the individual person and moved the paradigm more towards causation arising from the interaction of socially imposed restrictions. Both, nevertheless, assume that disabled people want to achieve some form of rehabilitation to normality and the rebuilding of old certainties. These ideas of a return to normality have increasingly come under attack as the disabled people's movement has grown in confidence:

> this is not just a matter of semantics but a concerted attempt to reject the normalising society. That some organisations of disabled people have not fully succeeded cannot be explained only as a matter of dispute between different political positions within the disability movement but also evidence of just how ingrained and deep-rooted the ideology of normality is within social consciousness more generally. (Oliver 1996b, p. 44)

It is also worth remembering that some people may have an impairment or disability without necessarily viewing themselves as disabled, particularly when the effects of their impairment can be reduced or controlled. For example, a person who has a slight degree of hearing loss may be said to have an impairment, but need not necessarily see themselves, or be perceived as, disabled because they can adopt strategies to minimise the social effects that turn an impairment into a disability. On a scale of hearing impairment they might be ranked at the opposite end of the scale from a profoundly deaf person. If all forms of impairment were quantified in terms of severity of restriction of 'normal' activities, impaired hearing might be viewed as less restrictive than some forms of physical or mental impairment. Thus the person in the example would now have two separate frames of reference by which they might not classify themselves, or be classified by others as 'disabled'. In similar fashion, where two people have the same form of impairment, one may not view themselves as disabled, while the other may.

This consideration of impairment and disability moves Disability Studies to a closer examination of rights and liberation. These dimensions are now more accepted as a legitimate area of discourse, although they have not emerged without the struggle of centuries of prejudice, particularly in the area of medicine. The emergence of any sort of recognition of civil rights, or participative collaboration with people with disabilities, is inextricably linked to the development of professional medicine. This includes the array of pseudo-medical professions that have also been spawned. A number of conceptual models dominate the development of Disability Studies owing to their clarity of interpretation. All are associated with phases of political, historical and economic development. The models have an explanatory power that is immediately understandable and accessible in relation to planning, organisation and practices around the expansion of rights and entitlement for disabled people.

Individual tragedy or medical model

Like so many other initiatives involving a group of people who have been marginalised, the beginnings of provision for people with disabilities is shrouded in some mystery. Nevertheless, from the outset it has involved the relationship of differential power between 'helpers' and 'helped', the demands of the labour market and the reification of the roles of those groups of individuals providing services.

Explanations of disability as personal tragedy for the person concerned have emerged from a long history. Rioux (1996) and Johnstone (1995) have indicated some of the sociological and psychological adaptations that tend to be made by non-disabled people in their adjustments towards disabled people in society. The medical model projects a dualism which tends to categorise the able-bodied as somehow 'better' or superior to people with disabilities. It shares much in common with the earlier taxonomy established by Kurtz (1964), with particular reference to people with learning difficulties. The image of disabled people is identified with pity, fear and charity and it is these considerations that contribute the explanatory power of such a hypothesis.

The theoretical explanation of the model relies on its legitimisation of the primitive fears associated with disability rather than any attempts at objective rigour:

Able bodied	versus	Disabled
Normal		Abnormal
Good		Bad
Clean		Unclean
Fit		Unfit
Able		Unable
Independent		Dependent

Such descriptions have been used to justify the assumption that it is legitimate to do things *to* people with disabilities rather than attempt to do things with them. Such explanations served as the rationale for large asylums and coercive control of disabled people in the guise of philanthropy that denied the right of reproduction to disabled people at the beginning of the twentieth century.

Yet, as has already been indicated, disabled people do not readily conform to a particular type. The creation of a taxonomy of categories does little to adequately represent the sheer diversity and range that makes up the population of people with disabilities. As Oliver (1990, p. 4) says about the medical model, 'it conserves the notion of impairment as abnormality in function, disability as not being able to perform an activity considered normal for a human being and handicap as the inability to perform a normal social role'.

Rioux (1996) has argued that such explanation of disability as a taxonomy of medical/biological problems has now grown and matured to encompass characteristics of disability as a service or social problem:

> Using this formulation, the hypothesis is that the deficit lies within the individual, but the concept of treatment is broadened to include both ameliorating the condition and developing ways to enable people to develop the potential they have. From this perspective there has been no attempt to reframe the notion that the problems experienced by people with disabilities are a result of their individual impairments. (Rioux 1996, p. 124)

What has come to be described as the 'medical' model emerged from the tendency of most of us to see medical services as the epitome of a powerful professional group. Doctors carry with them an aura of God-like responsibility over life and death. This reification in turn had a profound effect on the kinds of professional services received, the education and training provision made and also the manner in which these were implemented. This powerful influence suggests that, if a person has a disability, the medical model of causation implies that to all intents and purposes, 'It's your own fault!' As Oliver (1990) and Johnstone (1995) have pointed out, this pervasive influence from medicine is a major factor in the individualisation of 'care' issues.

It is not difficult to see how, from their beginnings, service-providers have defined the 'problem' of disablement as somehow the responsibility of disabled people themselves. For example the traditional function of the medical profession is to assess patient need, prescribe an intervention and facilitate a cure. It is as close as any of us get to playing the almighty. Disabled people have tended to collude with and to be dominated by this medically defined construct as much as anyone who is 'under the doctor'. The 'medical model' is deceptively simple. Nevertheless, when it is used as an explanation for society's response to impairment and disablement it can be seen to be problematic. The medical model is grounded firmly in the principles of normalisation, the return to 'wholeness' which is impossible to achieve (and may not be desired). The three elements of medical cure outlined in the model share many of the characteristics provided by other professional services:

- medical condition (symptoms)
- diagnosis/prescription
- cure or treatment

The model has an immediate appeal for the return of a bodily or sensory 'wholeness'. However, it is disingenuous when applied to disabled people who have, perhaps, been impaired since birth. It also emphasises the patient status and thereby carries assumptions of a required passivity from disabled people. The result is an emphasis on what disabled people cannot do and what disabled people will need if their lives are to function adequately with a particular medical condition. 'An assumption is made that disabled people function at a lower rate than an able-bodied person and that, in fact, a disabled person is inadequate' (Gillespie-Sells and Campbell 1991, p. 15). This in turn reinforces the cycle of prejudice and discrimination that so often accompanies the 'difficult' patient who fails to respond to treatment from the caring professional:

- failure (label)
- blame (low self-esteem and/or dependency on services)
- repeat presentation of symptoms to another specialist

The understanding of this concept of disability is premised on a shared understanding of normality. It clearly emphasises a power relationship in favour of the professionals and reinforces the personal tragedy theory of disablement. The subtle message of the medical model is that people with impairments and disabilities should be grateful for their treatment and that if there is a problem it is, in effect, the fault and responsibility of the patient for failing to follow the recommended intervention.

Rehabilitation model

The original meaning of the term 'rehabilitation' is associated with compensatory programmes to help people come to terms with their impairment and/or newly acquired disability. Rehabilitation, therefore, emphasises the restoration of a person's dignity and/or legal status. However, in recent years rehabilitation has begun to concentrate more on the interactions between people with disabilities and their environments and is becoming more multidisciplinary. The emphasis is upon the participation of individuals in making choices.

Rehabilitation is, thus, about facilitating adjustment to disability as well as community integration (Renwick and Friefeld 1996). The traditional rehabilitation model is based on a liberal interpretation of care for disabled people as 'restoration'. This pattern is beginning to disappear as statutory and voluntary agencies break away from the medical model. The medical interpretation of disability is, nevertheless, integral to rehabilitation with clear emphasis on personal care towards disabled people and an aim of restoration to approximately normal functioning individuals. This interpretation of 'normal' is linked to cultural expectations and what people were like before they became disabled. As has already been indicated, the model reinforces the belief that disabilities are caused by a health condition, such as a disease, a congenital malformation, a trauma, accident, or malnutrition. Once more it tends to emphasise personal tragedy and this is in marked contrast to the functional lifestyle of non-disabled people:

> A normally functioning person does not have to grapple with the social (or administrative) model of disability which is made up of a complex interrelationship of poor access, inadequate housing, insufficient income, cash starved social services and professional control over their lives. (Silburn 1993, p. 224)

In such administrative and professionally dominated circumstances it is worth remembering that care and charity can still be a form of rejection. Disabled people are not objects who merely receive services, they are also participants in the processes that shape their lives. Revolutions begin when people who are defined as problems achieve the power to redefine the problem. As McKnight (1995) points out, the hegemony of the professions will only be challenged when 'the client population' begin to question whether they really are the problem and start to recognise the limitations of professional help.

Social model

The medical model encourages the simplistic view that disability is a personal tragedy for the individuals concerned. It is disabled people who are seen to have, and may come to see themselves as having, 'needs'. The challenge and the strength of the social model of disability lies in its ability to reverse the emphasis of causation away from the individual and personal towards shared and collective responsibility. It is a theory founded on the premise that it is society that perpetuates the oppression and exclusion of people with disabilities. Thus, the onus of responsibility is shifted from the individual with an impairment or disability to the restrictions imposed by the construction of the environment and the attitudes of institutions and organisations.

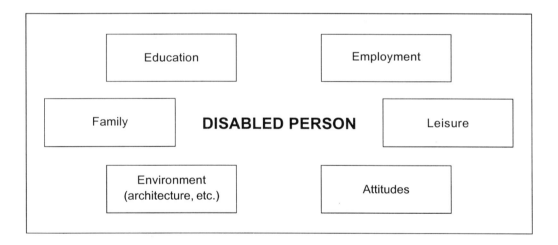

The essential difference between the medical and the social model of disability revolves around the shift in the explanatory power. The social model, unlike the medical, acknowledges the structural and personal barriers created by society. It also recognises the need for the participation of disabled people in decision making and the limitations of professional expertise. The elements of the social model can be summarised as follows:

- recognises the interaction of structural and attitudinal variables that create disability in society.
- recognises the voice/opinion of the disabled person.

- acknowledges the political processes that oppress and deny civil rights to disabled people.
- begins to put power/information within the control of disabled people and their organisations.

Criticisms of the social model of disability have begun to emerge since the beginnings of the 1990s. The social model has been blamed for being atheoretical, with no firm foundation of established scientific 'truth' against which it can be measured and tested. There are also the concerns raised by disabled people who have drawn attention to the reality that some impairments involve chronic and enduring pain and discomfort that can be relieved through medical interventions (Crow 1996). These criticisms are important, but unfortunately tend to undermine what has been a useful and accessible explanation for shifting both collective and individual thinking about disability issues. It is also rather presumptuous to believe that any one model can ever fully account for the social actions of human behaviour. By its nature, the social model has emerged from the lived experiences of disabled people in order to generate its illustrative power. As an explanation it must somehow begin to incorporate, rather than stand in opposition to, the medical/deficit model of disablement. In other words the bureaucracy and limitations indicated by the medical model can be seen to form part of the institutional limitations that are fundamental to the social model of disability.

Some people may be affected by more than one form of impairment, but may only feel themselves to be disabled by one of these. Thus, for example, a person with asthma, hearing loss and arthritis may find that their asthma can be controlled by medication, and that the provision of a hearing aid may give them sufficiently adequate hearing to cope with most situations, but if they cannot walk up steps and stairs they are disabled by the interaction of arthritis and the built environment. Generalising about disability is further complicated by the range and variety in the severity of the effects of forms of impairment. Throughout the research literature on disability it is apparent that for some people their level of disability has increased and is likely to continue to do so, whilst for others there is no pattern of deterioration. In many cases people have 'good days and bad days' and they live their lives accordingly.

The social model, nevertheless, appears to be grounded in liberal rather than radical conceptions of equal opportunities. It thereby suffers from some of the weaknesses associated with this paradigm (e.g. excess bureaucratisation at the point of decision making and an emphasis on fairness being perceived as individual rather than collective justice). A more radical conception of social justice within disability politics has come to be associated with a rights-based model.

Rights based model

The examination of rights and entitlements moves the discourse of Disability Studies into an exploration of the tensions between the private and public arenas of equal opportunities. This suggests that the politicisation of disability as personal experience needs to be articulated within a theory of equal opportunities. The narrowly private world of the individual and the personal circumstances of disabled people are not sufficient as explanations. What is required in a rights-based explanation is an articulation of the publicly accountable provision made for and received by disabled people as a movement.

The rights-based model of disability has thus emerged as a more politicised extension of the social model of disability. It began to emerge as a phenomenon in the late 1950s and early 1960s in Western Europe and the United States and has been articulated by a variety of groups at the margins of an increasingly consumer-driven society. The battles for legislation to outlaw discrimination against various groups in society – women, gays and lesbians, black people and, most recently, disabled people – have been and are being fought separately, but the underlying issues are the same. The rights-based model attempts to address some fundamental considerations that are grounded in equal opportunity theory:

- that all persons have a right to self-determination;
- that psychological and social conditions of freedom cause some individuals and groups to experience unfair advantages in determining their future;
- that declines in prospects for self-determination for the less fortunate are due to social forces beyond their control;
- that as a result there is a collective obligation to improve prospects for self-determination for less well-situated groups.

It has only been in recent years that the discourse around disability has turned to a consideration of human rights. Human rights, in their turn, have been influenced by the growing strength of the disability movement and the emerging self-confidence of disabled people. A rights-based discourse spreads the dimensions of disablement to include civil, political, economic, social, cultural and environmental obligations. These rights are enshrined in a number of international charters and declarations and they should be applied to everyone. An example of rights is that developed by the Universal Declaration of Human Rights, or the United Nations Declaration on the Rights of Disabled Persons (for extracts from these charters see Disability Awareness in Action 1993, pp. 40–55).

The rights-based model expands the social model of disability by moving the emphasis for change away from individuals to the requirement for changes in the structure of society:

- It recognises the existence of structural discrimination against disabled people in society.
- It acknowledges the collective strength of people.
- The agenda is determined by disabled people and their allies.
- It recognises legislation as a basis for establishing the visibility of the democratically enforceable rights of disabled people.
- It brings legal sanction to any act of disability discrimination.

In the United Kingdom legislation has been used to challenge and outlaw discrimination on the grounds of 'race' and/or gender. These attempts at reform may not have been considered completely successful, but they have been used as a signal to encourage disabled people to demand similar legislation, with a major focus being on 'civil rights' rather than 'needs'. In so doing, disabled people are arguing for legislation that challenges and prevents the unfair discriminatory practices that exist both socially and institutionally, in both direct and indirect forms. While the Disability Discrimination Act 1995 (HMSO 1996) recognises some of these concerns it still perceives discrimination against disabled people as individually rather than collectively determined. Adherence to the state or, alternatively, the market for ensuring the maintenance of these rights is a substitute for the pluralist and inclusive democracy which, it is argued, an effective rights-based model of disablement implies.

Even those who have supported the enabling legislation of the Disability Discrimination Act see it as only a partially effective tool in outlawing discrimination against disabled people. In a range of arenas, within employment, transport and access to goods and services, it tends to favour a gradual path towards equality as a virtue. One major criticism is that there is a general vagueness around some of the terms and conditions laid down. Many requirements are qualified by references to what is 'reasonable', which it is argued greatly diminishes the effectiveness of the legislation. Another criticism is the protracted time-scale over which the Act will be fully implemented. Some clauses (e.g. with regard to public transport) may not come into force until the second decade of the twenty-first century.

From needs to rights and entitlements

Major influences concerning the development of rights for disabled people are still emerging. From the United States the cause of black rights has acted as a catalyst for other groups, including disabled people (Bynoe *et al.* 1991). The black civil rights movement has been fundamental in its influence on disabled people for a number of reasons:

- It re-conceptualised unequal treatments of marginalised groups into a more appropriate political context of equal opportunities and human rights. Rather than a human tragedy and therefore, an individual 'problem', the cause was seen as a public and political concern.
- It demonstrated the possibility of achieving social change within a society. It also galvanised all people, who until then had overlooked their own role in the construction and perception of disability and special needs as a 'problem'.

The campaigns have all tended to come to successful fruition as a consequence of direct action and political activism. The Americans with Disabilities Act 1990 (Morrissey 1991) is an example of legislation that has come to be a powerful testimony to the campaigning zeal of disabled people. It is also a symbol of, and justification for, political activity in the development of civil rights for people with disabilities in other parts of the world. However, in the United Kingdom the evidence that disabled people are still denied their full rights to citizenship is overwhelming. It seems evident that, despite political rhetoric to the contrary, 'social disadvantage' has become associated with disability and that young people with disabilities are cases to be treated rather than individuals with rights.

It is only recently that commentators have begun to question if the very services set up to help establish a better quality of life may not instead be helping to create the problems they were designed to resolve. Bureaucratic assessment procedures and the perpetuation of segregated and residential facilities have denied people the right to live where they choose. The intersection of disability, community provision for disabled people and inclusive living is crucial, particularly in terms of the realisation of individual potential (see Johnstone 1995).

Summary

In this chapter Disability Studies is discussed as a multi-disciplinary subject area that sets out to explore both the private and the collective experiences of disabled people. The differences between the labels of disability, impairment and handicap are outlined and critically analysed. The strongly medical definitions that are associated with the individual 'tragedy' of an impairment, e.g. chronic loss, pain, loss of status, are compared with the more politicised social construction of disability. The contrasts between these two simple models are emphasised. The emergence of a language discourse that empowers and liberates disabled people as a group, in a more inclusive paradigm of marginalisation and oppression, is discussed. Shared oppression is argued as a liberating feature of the disability movement. This brings attention to an explanation of disability based on the demand for civil rights. This has grown as numbers of disabled people have started to act collectively in order to seek access to civic rights and full citizenship. This, in turn, forms the basis for a critical examination of community care and forms the backdrop for the exploration of equal opportunities in Chapter 2.

Critical factors in community care and independent living

Questions

- Is it necessary to set the issue of disability within an equal opportunities context?
- Do you regard it as a professional duty or an invasion of privacy to make decisions on behalf of people with disabilities?
- Should Disability Studies be concerned with raising issues that deal with conflict and prejudice?
- What do you see as the main tensions in the concept of independent living?

Introduction

The explanations of disability outlined in Chapter 1 can be viewed as the beginnings of a theoretical framework for the status of disabled people in society. This chapter sets out to critically examine the complexity of the service provision developed to meet the needs of disabled people and some of the attitudes associated with service provision. Too often the very services intended to bring disabled and non-disabled people closer have had the contrary effect of sustaining the marginalisation of disabled people – the very thing they are aiming to dispel. Finkelstein (1979, p. 7) summarises this paradox as follows:

> All those working in the field of disability and earning their livelihood from this occupation are dependent on the existence of a never-ending disabled client market. They are part of the disability complex. The contention here is that the experience of the helper side of the disability relationship makes possible the generation of specific attitudes towards

'disability'. One particular characteristic of these attitudes is that, since they emerge from the 'helper' (or able bodied) side of the relationship, they focus exclusively on the 'helped' side. Because the 'helpers' are the articulators of how disability should be described and presented to the public, these one-sided attitudes are taken as representative of the totality – of attitudes towards disability itself.

Just as we cannot really be surprised that people with disabilities continue to see themselves as undervalued, we should also not be surprised when we see professional carers and educators as the 'needs providers'. For example, students and children emerging from special education courses continue to consider themselves to be 'in need' and often, thereby, requiring the benefits of charitable and statutory services. However, having a disability or an impairment is not the same thing as having 'needs'. It is often because people have been socialised into accepting the definition of disability as a personal tragedy that the concept of 'need' emerges. Nevertheless, the media images associated with disabled people continue to be somewhat contradictory extremes. People with impairments are either pathetic victims, arch villains or heroes. The stereotype of the disabled child is either that of the brave little lost boy or girl overcoming personal tragedy, or, in later life, the scheming malcontent determined to have revenge on society for the misfortune that has befallen him or her. Other alternative examples of disabled people who have become public figures have tended to overlook the part that impairment has played in their lives, e.g. President Roosevelt, David Blunkett or Frank Williams.

The need for disability

The 'industry of concern' that has grown to serve the needs of disabled people has resulted in an increased sense of professional protection amongst the services created. The growth of professional services in Western economies has seen the shift from manufacturing to service industries and has created the need to redefine employment in its wake. Each year fewer people are employed to produce goods and therefore there is a need to create something else for people to do. The liberal ideal of caring and the market-led notions of efficiency have come alarmingly close together. There is a growing belief that the production of a service as a capital 'good', which can contribute to the gross national product of a country's economy, equates with the industry of a factory that produces a motor car. However, when an economy is based primarily on the production of services, the essential new material is people who are in need or who are deficient: 'Just as General Motors needs steel, a service economy *needs* "deficiency", "human problems" and "needs" if it is to grow . . . . The economic need for need creates a demand for redefining conditions of deficiency' (McKnight 1995, p. 29).

So, in effect, the industry of disability perpetuates the dependency it has been created to resolve. The caring services, researchers and academics that form the disability 'industry' redefine themselves and the concept of disablement, but cannot afford to get rid of disability itself.

Disability as inequality

We are seeing in the emergence of Disability Studies a resurgence of interest in the fundamental principle of how people should be treated. The disability movement, individual disabled people and their advocates are beginning to question if the services developed to promote a satisfactory quality of life are in fact adequate. These questions go to the heart of the meaning of social justice and raise issues of what it means to receive a fair share of the 'national cake' of prosperity. The case of disability suggests that the way disabled people are perceived, measured and treated is far from ideal. Rioux (1996) has indicated that the dominance of the medical model has created an identifiable hierarchy within the social construction of disability and also in the determination of equality.

- A person is labelled or distinguished from others in such a way that he or she is considered as socially inferior;
- Care and treatment, including professional standards and practice, law policy and political rights, are developed and legitimated on the basis of this label of social inferiority;
- A paternalistic denial of liberties and self-determination is imposed, premised on the social obligation that attaches to the status.

And through such methods, intentional or otherwise, the cycle of oppression remains unbroken.

Disability as need: the case of special education

The concept of 'need' first emerged in education in 1946, in regulations that indicated how to implement the 1944 Education Act. These regulations led to the establishment of services and schools that acted on behalf of, rather than in consultation with, disabled people. This, in turn, has led, until recently, to a kind of passive citizenship on the part of disabled people within a fundamentally needs-based provision determined by educational profession-als. The legal framework of the UK has consistently portrayed the education of disabled people as a cost to the exchequer rather than as an individual's entitlement to participate in the exercise of citizenship. Indeed, such has been the determination to see special education as an extension of a form of treat-ment, that we have only in the last fifteen years started to dismantle a special education system that deliberately excluded pupils and students with special educational needs from participation in the 'ordinary' school curriculum.

A feature of the 1944 Act was the creation of categories of handicap reflect-ing society's needs rather than individual considerations. Regulations in Pamphlet 5, following the Act, actually stated that some pupils may require special educational 'treatment', borrowing heavily from the medical model already referred to. For young people with handicaps and disabilities, leaving school meant a probable future in sheltered or closed employment. Even in 1968 it was estimated that there were approximately 70,000 severely mentally handicapped adults in England and Wales, approximately 24,500 of whom attended Adult Training Centres (Whelan and Speake 1977). The need to re-establish employment for returning members of the armed forces follow-ing the Second World War had the effect of excluding disabled individuals from open employment, even though some of them had fulfilled important work during the war years.

The much more specific definition of learning difficulties within the concept 'Special Educational Needs' formed part of the legal framework of the 1981 Education Act and followed from the recommendations put forward by the Warnock Committee of Enquiry in 1978 (Warnock 1978). This Act has in turn been replaced by the 1993 Education Act and its accompanying Code of Practice (DfEE 1994). As Booth (1992) has argued, the implications of the definitions are that children and students are to be measured using both 'within the individual' measures, e.g. standard tests of intelligence or abil-ity (which, in themselves, suggest measuring the incompetence or failure of a person as the basis of learning difficulties) and, secondly, 'environmental judgements' of the adequacy or otherwise of the resources available to facili-tate and support teaching and learning. The whole concept of 'need' is problematic and confusing. For children in schools, it has led to an increase in services established for the purpose of meeting individual need and providing support. It is only recently that some commentators have begun to question whether the very services set up to help establish better learning may not, instead, be helping to create the problems they were designed to resolve (Booth 1992; Corbett and Barton 1992; Johnstone 1995).

The fundamentally child-centred ideas of the Warnock Report attempted to establish a concept of citizenship by building on the notion of need, determined by the collaboration of 'experts' and through the wider integration of children from segregated educational provision into the mainstream. In fact, it failed to alter many of the old prejudices. Had the original recommendations, for the education of all children in ordinary schools, been more adequately resourced, the current arguments for and against inclusion might not have become so strident. The present philosophical shift towards inclusive education is itself an acknowledgement that full integration is an ideal that may not ultimately be completely achievable, or even desired for everyone with a disability. But inclusion does acknowledge that it is the structures of the education system that have to change, rather more than trying to attempt to fit an individual to the system. More than anything else, however, the concept of inclusion stresses the emphasis on rights. The concept of special educational needs has, until now, failed to face up to the fundamental issue of ensuring that basic educational rights are part of every child's entitlement. As Johnstone (1995) points out, Special Educational Need has become such an abused and misunderstood term that it has diminished two perfectly honourable and worthwhile concepts, 'Care' and 'Need', which have fundamentally influenced the creation of the term in the first place. The system of meeting a child or student's 'needs' has continued to perpetuate some of the worst abuses of the old models of medical care through the imposition of bureaucratic assessment procedures on young people and their families and the perpetuation of segregated educational and residential facilities which deny the right for some people to live where they choose. This in turn has denied them any feelings of 'normality'.

The move towards inclusion

The relationship between community provision for disabled people and the economy is seen in the original 'philanthropic' ideals that lay behind the development of a structured system of provision in the institutions and 'colonies' that were established in both Europe and the United States in the nineteenth century. In some areas of the United Kingdom they continued to form the basis for residential care until the shift in policy during the 1970s towards 'Care in the Community'. Some semi-formal education and vocational training for people with disabilities and learning difficulties had been an established feature of the asylums of the nineteenth century. The development of activities for young men and women with disabilities and psychiatric disorders in the asylums of the nineteenth century has been interestingly described by a visitor to the Earlswood Asylum situated just outside London:

It was in furthering the many schemes for the improvement of idiots, a most important object to enable those capable of reaping the highest advantages, to become adept in some useful branch of industry, and to make their work remunerative, exchanging their solitary and idle habits for social, industrious and productive occupation. (*Edinburgh Review* 1865, p. 56)

This paternalistic approach was soon to be replaced by the harsher, more custodial activities associated with asylums as arenas for the protection of society, rather than as places of refuge for disabled people. In the 'Moral Panic' that developed around eugenics, the populist demand grew for the asylums to become places of custody. This meant a shift in emphasis; from training individuals in order to protect them from threats and exploitation from the rest of society, to the protection of society from the supposed debilitating effects of physically, intellectually (and, by association, morally) inadequate people. Any understanding of shared responsibility for either the causation or the resolution of these circumstances was quite clearly overlooked.

The overarching perception of rights for disabled people has emerged at the same time as debates about choice and opportunities for the integration, or inclusion, of minority populations as part of an almost global social policy. Scandinavian society has led the way in promoting non-segregation for all groups of people.

Soder (1980), writing at around the same time as the policy initiative for changes in special education in the United Kingdom (for example, the Warnock Report of 1978), has provided operational definitions of integration that divide it into four main groups:

(i) Physical integration, i.e. the physical (or geographical) distance between the handicapped and non-handicapped is reduced. This is the most common form of integration of handicapped young people in Sweden, which means segregated classrooms in ordinary school and college buildings.

(ii) Functional integration, i.e. the functional distance is reduced. This means that handicapped and non-handicapped students are using the same educational equipment and resources. In turn the functional integration can be divided into two branches, where co-utilization (which can be simultaneous or non-simultaneous) means that students only share material and co-operation means planned common activities.

(iii) Social integration, i.e. the social distance is reduced. This means that the handicapped person forms part of a community with non-handicapped persons and comes into regular and spontaneous contact with these.

(iv) Societal integration, i.e. the adult handicapped person has the same access to resources and opportunity to influence his own situation as others; he has a productive working role and forms part of a social community with others.

(Soder 1980, pp. 10–11)

This hierarchy of form has been expanded by others who have added additional sophistication rather than radically altering Sodor's original four-step model, e.g. a fifth level has been termed 'personal integration' and is given the following definition:

Personal integration is related to the developing and changing needs for personal interaction with significant persons. It includes the opportunities to have a satisfactory private life with meaningful relationships, for example for the child: parents, siblings, relatives and friends; and for the adult: relatives, friends, marriage partner and children. (Nirje 1980, p. 48)

Some problems with this concept of integration have already been alluded to, but they have been subject to a good deal of critical scrutiny. Definitions of integration fit well with the widely developed construct of 'normalisation' and clearly have links with the debate about 'quality of life'. But it is interesting to note that the most common forms of integration and inclusiveness in educational and community settings remain at the lower end of the hierarchy. This raises a number of questions about the appropriateness of applying levels to a concept that is in a proper sense indivisible. As Rosenqvist (1993) has pointed out, in a wholeness no exclusions are possible, since everybody is needed in forming this wholeness: 'if someone is taken away the wholeness has lost some of its contributions and is thus spoiled.'

The implementation of integration reforms in educational settings have shown that social goals are not always realised. Various studies have indicated that people with disabilities establish very few relationships with non-handicapped young people and that those people who have been encouraged to integrate socially often appear to become excluded even in the integrated setting (e.g. Johnstone 1995). This tension between the ideals of full inclusion and the reality of only partial success has been partly attributed to the lack of social networks that are available to people with disabilities. The closure of large institutions in favour of enclave housing is an example of the expectations that people with disabilities, and particularly those with more severe learning difficulties, will begin to establish social relations with non-handicapped people. This optimistic expectation assumes that society is ready to accept the integration of disabled and non-disabled people as unproblematic. In fact, the reality is that in the worst cases isolation has increased as large institutions have been replaced by smaller ones.

This shift towards addressing disability within a political framework of rights and entitlements has been part of a process that has been given its lead in the world of further education. As has been pointed out, special education is in danger of being perceived as focussed on shallow judgements of individual needs as selected needs and the business of access to buildings and the curriculum (Corbett and Barton 1992; Johnstone 1995). Rather than this, it should be considered as an issue to be studied with a proper examination of both the institutional and structural inequalities inherent in society. If, by so doing, we place the exploration of disability and special education within the context of equal opportunities, it then becomes part of a more fundamental contribution to civic awareness.

In 1995 I suggested that the development of inclusive provision for people with disabilities in the United Kingdom had become a player in a larger political poker game. I am now inclined towards another party game of 'Pass the Parcel'. Thus, the concerns of disabled people have taken the form of an economic and class debate around poverty, 'family values' and 'back to basics'. Any attempt to influence change in provision for people with disabilities now has to recognise the additional responsibilities of engaging in political challenge, not simply seeking to affect legislation. The challenge is inherent in the language of debate as well as the agenda for action. In order to influence the structures of power and control in the development of services, the debates and judgements will have to be in terms of 'rights' rather than 'needs'. This may well involve the uncomfortable acknowledgement that most of the injustices towards disabled people have emerged from, and are still located in, a system that talks of change but does little to resolve its own practices. This sense of inequity and injustice needs to touch the lives of the vast majority, and not solely people with disabilities, in order to bring real change.

The criticisms applied to education are equally applicable to other forms of service provision for disabled people. Provision is dominated by the notion that disabled people are in need of care. Professionals tend to deal in 'needs' and 'care'. Disabled people often prefer to talk about 'personal assistance', rejecting the association between care and dependency. One key demand is that instead of being provided with services, which are not necessarily tailored to individual requirements, those who wish should receive cash payments to purchase assistance privately. Government policy has prevented local authorities from participating in such schemes (Oliver 1996b). In those parts of the country where it has been possible, e.g. Hampshire, this has been found to be successful by many people, and its availability nationally will do much to liberate disabled people from the constraints of bureaucracy.

It should be emphasised, however, that I do not wish to imply that one potential form of oppression (service provision) should be replaced by another potentially oppressive practice (disabled people being forced to purchase care, manage their care budget, etc.), but that both options should be available. The struggles by disabled people to reclaim control of their own lives have shifted the debate away from the concept of 'need' to issues around the right to participate, which is, arguably, one of the key issues of the 1990s.

The right to employment

The comfortable certainties and routines of childhood are intended to serve as a preliminary to the often more informal and haphazard aspects of life as an adult. One of the most inclusive, and until the 1980s and 1990s, ordinary things about adult life is employment. It is therefore no surprise that many of our formative childhood and 'pretend' experiences are related to jobs. In similar fashion, education and training have been expected to accommodate the expectations of employers in preparing young people for the job market; by developing personal and social skills, craft skills and qualifications as prerequisites for securing employment.

Some of the benefits of paid employment are obvious. As has been pointed out, people have defined themselves by their work throughout this century:

> They were miners, engineers, printers, draymen, tanners. And they were predominantly male. But as the manufacturing industries collapsed, more jobs were taken by women and millions of badly educated men could no longer define themselves. 'I'm a printer' could be said with pride; 'I'm on benefit' is a mark of exclusion. (Hugill 1997, p. 29)

The combination of social interaction and feelings of self-worth that employment and the process of task completion can provide apply equally to people with disabilities. Some of the benefits of a job can be usefully summarised as follows:

- A job provides economic independence and a better standard of living.
- A job can empower people, by enabling them to become self-determining rather than living their lives as others dictate.
- A job provides status that influences positive attitudes towards disabled people and public visibility.
- Workplaces in integrated settings provide opportunities for social interaction and friendships.
- A job is one of the ways in which the majority of people continue to learn and develop skills, competences and intellectual abilities.
- Work gives our lives a routine and structure. Successful employment

and job satisfaction gives people a sense of fulfillment, achievement, confidence and dignity.

- Developing employment opportunities is cost-effective. A job involves people exercising their independence and choice to become self-supporting, rather than remaining dependent upon a lifetime of support services.

So, just as it is recognised that all people including those with disabilities can benefit from employment, it is also recognised that in a more competitive environment some people will require additional support if employment is to take place. In the past five years in the UK all political parties have taken to advising the unemployed and the disabled that they should take some responsibility for the circumstances they are in. Education and training are seen as the key to overcoming the skills deficit in the work force. Griffiths (1990), commenting in relation to people with severe learning difficulties, claims that too often, too little is expected of people with learning difficulties and that, given suitable training and help, they are capable of working in both sheltered and open employment. The under-expectation that he has highlighted is a carry-over from the protectiveness felt towards people deemed to be vulnerable. But whereas most people grow to assert their rights, many people with disabilities remain passive and inarticulate in the face of the often well-meaning but ultimately oppressive will of others.

There are a number of significant factors which continue to act as barriers to open employment for people with disabilities. The most fundamental is the structural unemployment and under-employment arising from the skills revolution. This means that employers are demanding a work force that is articulate, adaptable and innovative, rather than tied to the manual labour of the production line. The supply of jobs available is clearly related to the structural characteristics of the local economy, but it is also dependent upon the nature of work itself. This particularly affects the relationship between people with disabilities and the attitudes of employers and fellow employees.

The tendency to have an undifferentiated view of disabled people as a homogeneous group operates in the workplace as well as other areas of life. This means that people with disabilities, and learning difficulties in particular, are held in low regard. Too often they are thought capable of undertaking only repetitive and 'simple' tasks, and if such work does not exist then a person with a disability will not be considered as employable. Such issues are particularly pertinent in connection with jobs where 'initiative' is seen as a prerequisite for work. In the same way that special education can mean streamed or segregated provision, special work placements can become discrete enclaves set in sheltered settings where imagination and initiative on the part of supervisors, disabled employees and their workmates is neither required nor encouraged. Attendance in these 'closed' settings limits opportunities for social experiences and any access to wider opportunities for employment promotion or changes to working practice that are usually an anticipated part of working life.

Equality of opportunity for access to employment has become a policy objective for a range of disadvantaged and under-represented groups. Nevertheless, the changing nature of Britain and the diminishing manufacturing base of the country has affected employment opportunities for everyone. The decline of manufacturing has coincided roughly with a technological revolution that has reduced the need for an unskilled workforce or even low levels of skill in the labour market. Training and education initiatives have been given an ideological steer in an attempt to restructure the political and economic fortunes of the country. As has been noted, doubts about the potency of economic performance have confronted all governments and employers in late twentieth century technological societies. As training has delayed and in some cases replaced entry to paid employment, an increasing number of young people have become alienated from what is perceived to be a hierarchy of education and training outcomes. Educational achievement has become even more important as the first indication of the transition to adult entitlement and ultimately to the workplace. A reconsideration of the purpose of education and training has become fundamental for most people in order to gain entry to any sort of employment or income above mere subsistence level. These issues are exacerbated for people with disabilities who are socially disadvantaged at the point of developing a career, for a number of reasons. As Johnstone (1995) has commented, educational and vocational training programmes can appear to disadvantage young adults with disabilities, as can other initiatives developed as pre-employment initiatives. It has been apparent that some people can stay for years within a cycle of different, but badly coordinated, training schemes (Finn 1997; Kennedy 1997). They never actually achieve either adequate qualification or ultimate paid employment. Of those who achieve a qualification, most show only modest results. The majority, who receive special certificates or records of achievement related to elements within their training, have a qualification that still has little currency with employers. As a result, there are a number of unskilled and unqualified people fit for low-paid employment and they are always under threat of being laid off at short notice. Young women in this category are doubly disadvantaged, either staying at home on completion of their formal schooling, or obtaining a job that earns them so little that independent living is impossible.

The factor of age and disability

The associations between disability and age are inescapable. As a critical variable in the study of disability, age can be thought of as the ticking time bomb that each of us carries with us. Just as loss has been portrayed as the dominant metaphor in the medical model of disablement and impairment, so it also informs and operationalises perspectives about the onset and impact of the ageing process.

Theories on ageing have tended to be dominated by the expectation that individuals should learn to accept the stage-related features of the life cycle (e.g. birth, childhood. adolescence, early adulthood, etc.). As Oliver reminds us, it is highly unlikely that any of us will reach the conclusion of our working lives without becoming more conscious of the effects of an impairment. People who grow old gracefully are assumed to be adapting normally to the ageing process. Thus, ageing has its own inevitable expectations and behaviours; 'from this perspective, successful adaptation to ageing is represented by an individual accepting the changes that he or she has experienced and ultimately accepting the inevitability of death' (Oliver 1996a, p. 134).

The point in the life cycle at which disablement occurs may well be crucial. People who become disabled in old age may find their situation particularly difficult owing to the fact that they frequently have multiple impairments. For example, the elderly person who starts to go deaf may also be blind or have an arthritic condition. However, as French (1992) reminds us, it is important not to be ageist. Many older people cope with impairment and disability as effectively as younger people. An impairment incurred later in life, after one has established a social and economic position, has a different meaning and significance from the sense of loss experienced as a young adult. There is research that suggest that disability contracted in old age is considered part of the natural staged process of the life cycle (Zarb 1993a, 1993b). The OPCS survey (Martin et al. 1988) also confirms the association between disability and old age. The census had defined disability in relation to the inability to perform particular activities. Of the six million people living in Great Britain with at least one form of disablement, almost 70 per cent of disabled adults were aged 60 and over (Martin et al. 1988, p. 27). The very old emerged as those most likely to be affected, with 63 per cent of women and 53 per cent of men over the age of 75 being described as disabled. When severity is taken into account, the very old again predominated, with 64 per cent of adults in the two highest categories being 70 or over and 41 per cent aged 80 or over. Census data, nevertheless, suggests that the combination of an ageing population and new medical interventions which prolong life will ensure that the number of people with an impairment or chronic illness will increase significantly in the next two decades (see e.g. McEwen 1990).

Whilst the pain of an acquired impairment is no less real, it can be argued that a disability incurred at birth may be a 'first order' marker dominating one's identity, whilst an acquired disability that arises in old age is a subordinate one. In other words, the process of ageing and the onset of disablement are characterised by an element of 'disengagement' associated with behavioural changes and a decrease in the extent of people's social interactions.

This concept of the inevitability of decline and decrepitude, which is associated with individual pathology, can be criticised on a number of grounds:

- It perceives ageing as a negative experience, inevitably linked to death.
- It presupposes that chronic pain and disease predominate as both the cause of disability and the natural corollary of old age. Many disorders can be linked to later life, especially arthritis, hearing loss and declining eyesight. However, they should not be confused with the trauma, and congenital conditions, associated with disablement in the earlier years of life. Neither should they be considered to be inevitable. There are a number of reasons put forward to challenge the inevitability of disability associated with age.
- No account is taken of the social factors which are external to individuals; e.g. the reduction of social activity as people grow older is more likely to be linked to inadequate financial resources than the ageing process *per se*. Zarb (1993a, p. 55) has noted in his research how ageing with a disability is associated with increases in satisfaction for some individuals and decreases for others. For people who already experience disability, the onset of the ageing process has been described as a 'second disability'.

The idea that disablement is a medical problem which affects only a small proportion of the population of the aged can no longer be sustained. Internationally there are around 50 million disabled people in Europe (Daunt 1991) and approximately 500 million worldwide (Disabled People's International 1992). The combination of an ageing population and new medical interventions which prolong life is bound to ensure that the number of people with an 'impairment' or 'chronic illness' will increase substantially over the next few years. Attitudes held towards old people and the very definition of what it means to be old will thus need to be reconsidered.

The emergence of 'community care'

Towards the end of the 1970s the concept of 'community care' was emerging as the preferred alternative to institutionalised service provision. For feminist writers it presented a potential problem in that the family was identified as the location within which this community-based care would be provided and that the 'burden', therefore, was likely to fall on women (see Finch and Groves 1983; Beardshaw 1988). One major drawback in the planning of 'community care' is that it has assumed that families will continue to provide care. Community care has been presented as the ideal form of provision on the grounds of cost-effectiveness, moral responsibility (family members have a duty to care for one another) and as a safeguard against the abuse of individuals that may occur in institutional settings. The 'community care' bandwagon continued to gain momentum throughout the 1980s. The National Health Service and Social Services became separated and there was subsequent criticism of the fragmentary nature of service provision. The Griffiths Report of 1988 identified the role of Social Services as an enabling body rather than a service-provider. In keeping with current government policies, Social Services Departments were to make use of both private and voluntary sectors in purchasing services, and this was adopted in the 1990 National Health Service and Community Care Act (Morris 1993).

It was assumed that individuals would be assessed by a case manager and that a 'package of care' in terms of the necessary services would be purchased. Ultimately it was for Social Services to determine whether an individual's needs could be best met in the community or by residential care. Between 1991 and 1993 the Act was implemented, with the setting up of complaints and inspection units, the development of Community Care Plans (involving health and social service planners) and the separating of purchasing and providing services, together with the transfer from Social Security to local authority of residential care finance (Morris 1993).

Morris acknowledges the potential for good of the community care reforms but remains concerned about the unequal power relationship between professionals and disabled individuals. Services depend on assess-ment. Professionals, to a large extent, decide what is required and who will provide it, how and when. Morris, however, is firmly committed to the notion of direct payments, under which individuals would receive and man-age their own budgets, being responsible for 'hiring and firing' their own assistants. Although there was strong resistance to this, the government view is now more favourable.

Since the implementation of the community care reforms there has been a gradual shift in focus to include the views of service users. Community Care Plans are put out to consultation, with individuals and organisations being encouraged to make known their opinions. Some health and social care planners use the term 'consumer' or 'customer' rather than 'user', but Wilson (1996) argues that 'user' is the most accurate term, since the other two imply a level of voluntarism that is not necessarily true. In many cases people have little or no choice about services and very few people are in the position of paying in full for such services; therefore they are not customers, although possibly reluctant consumers.

The monitoring of services and policy outcomes is an area that is currently the focus of much investigation (Quereshi and Nocon 1996). Clearly it is important which service users are approached and how their views are recorded. Generally and historically, users have been unequal participants in the community care process and many may find it difficult to take part in the formal settings in which views are often sought. At the same time they may be dependent on services and fearful of giving offence by complaining. In this context there is a need for development work with users, both as groups and as individuals. User involvement is a crucial element in the struggles of disabled people and those who support them. (See Beresford and Harding 1993 for examples of and suggestions regarding the development of user-led services.)

Summary

A number of variables can be distinguished as markers that highlight the inequalities experienced by disabled people and their families. The Victorian charitable association between the 'deserving' and the 'undeserving' has moved in the 1980s and 1990s towards distinctions between the 'helpable' and the 'unhelpable' and the effectiveness or otherwise of welfare as a solution to structural unemployment. This in turn has highlighted one of the factors in society that is associated with disablement and lack of moral cohesiveness; an inadequate resource base for many services. The exclusion of disabled people from involvement in society's mainstream is demonstrated in education, employment and the services established to meet the requirements of 'care in the community'. Disablement is exacerbated by the poverty which emerges from poor employment prospects, limited educational opportunity and the inadequate structure of the welfare benefits system. The power of change through legislation forms the basis for the next chapter.

CHAPTER 3

Legislation in the UK and the USA

Questions

- Is there a constituency of disabled people that can influence change? Have disabled people a shared cultural identity?
- Are disabled people politically active? Will legislation bring more problems and serve to split the 'movement' towards social justice? Does it place unrealistic expectations on disabled people to litigate?
- Does anybody in society have rights? Where are the responsibilities that go with rights?
- Whose rights are ultimately being reinforced by legislation?

Introduction

The law plays an important symbolic and practical role in forming the ideological systems that legitimise specific sets of values and assumptions in society. It is, therefore, fundamental in forming the framework within which both groups and individuals interpret their participation in society (Gooding 1994). However, the traditional assumptions that the law does not discriminate has to be questioned. Although appearing impartial and neutral, the officers of the law and the judiciary are subject to the same prejudices as those from whom they are meant to stand apart. 'Precisely because of law's power to define, it is acknowledged to be an important site of struggle and resource for groups seeking social change' (Gooding 1994, p. 30).

The emerging legislation of the United Kingdom, in relation to social justice for people with disabilities, reflects a number of shifts in public policy towards the participation of disabled people in both employment and daily life. The speed of change is a reflection of the new group consciousness and political activism of disabled people and their own preparedness to use the law in order to shift public opinion away from perceptions of disabled people as 'defective' and incapable of full participation in the activities of daily living. Legislative change in relation to the rights of disabled people has occurred most significantly in the United Kingdom and the United States. It is recognised that the Americans with Disabilities Act has played a formative role in increasing the employment opportunities of disabled people in the USA and reduced their dependence on government entitlements (Blanch 1994). It has been anticipated that similar changes in the attitudes of both employers and wider society will emerge from the Disability Discrimination Act 1995 in the UK. However, prejudice and a reluctance to shift away from the intolerance and low expectations that many people still hold about disabled people may frustrate these burgeoning attempts at independence. When this is combined with the old-fashioned interpretations of the social welfare system in the United Kingdom and the exhaustion or 'greying' of the leadership within the disability movement, it is all the more problematic.

Discrimination and disabled people

The discrimination encountered by disabled people is not simply a question of individual prejudice, although that clearly occurs. Rather, it is institutionalised in the structures of society. Institutional discrimination is evident when the policies and activities of all types of organisations result in sustaining the inequalities between disabled people and non-disabled people. As indicated in Chapter 1, disabled people have been deliberately excluded from many aspects of community life, and Western culture is replete with disablist imagery and language which keep alive the traditional fears and prejudices surrounding impairment. The centrality of these judgements of 'difference' applies to the marginalisation of all discriminated-against groups. But they are particularly clearly marked in relation to the accounts of disabled people in the United Kingdom.

Background to provision in the United Kingdom

Within the paternalistic welfare services and capitalist economy of the United Kingdom the individualism of the law is one of its distinctive features. It has already been suggested that capitalist law tends to regard the rights and duties of all individuals as 'equal before the law' in a legal system that claims to remain impartial. Gooding (1994) criticises these inclinations towards a formal equality model of the law, arguing that such a philosophy is fundamentally flawed. The structure of the legal system tends to be confrontational and to reduce people to the status of isolated individuals; it fails to redress the inherently discriminatory behaviour which the law has shaped and continues to sustain. The legislation that has been passed throughout the century has tended, in fact, to reinforce the marginality and rejection of disabled people rather than signal their liberation (Bynoe *et al.* 1990; Johnstone 1995, 1996a). It would be easy to catalogue the failures of 'permissive' legislation. Numerous acts have purported to include consultation with disabled people and to defend the right of disabled people to participate. Nevertheless, the framing of the legislation has contained so many get-out clauses, or is so loosely drafted, that it has been ignored, overridden or simply gone unchallenged.

Nearly all acts of parliament concerning disabled people have tended to reinforce the domination of the medical model and the perception of disability as illness. The notorious Mental Health Act of 1913 had identified those who were deemed 'moral imbeciles' in order to justify the removal to asylums of pregnant but unmarried young women. Some 60 years later the 1973 Chronically Sick and Disabled Persons Act set out to identify the incidence of disability and the needs of disabled people in each local authority of England and Wales. In both cases the expectation was that disabled people were incapable of providing their own protection, care and recreation. The paternalistic state was charged with the duty to care and take responsibility for meeting need. This has led to an ever-growing army of paid professionals and voluntary carers.

It has only been since the 1980s that the stifling grip of paternalistic law has been loosened. This was born not only out of an attempt by the government to address the discontent felt by disabled people after ten years of unsuccessful bids at legislation but also from a fear of parliamentary defeat on a private member's bill from the opposition – the Civil Rights (Disabled Persons) Bill. This bill was supported by the disability movement, but opposed by the Conservative ruling government at the time. This opposition arose from the belief that it would place too high a burden on businesses and would, thus, inhibit their abilities to compete in the economic market place. What has emerged is an act designed, as a form of political damage limitation, to be acceptable and yet economically cost-effective to implement.

The legal basis of provision in the United Kingdom

> A person has a disability if he has a physical or mental impairment which has a substantial long term adverse effect on his ability to carry out normal day to day activities. (Disability Discrimination Act 1995, p. 1)

The Disability Discrimination Act (1995) received Royal Assent on 8 November 1995 and now forms the main focus for ending discrimination against disabled people in the United Kingdom. After a number of years of argument about its purpose and above all its costs, the Act has established the following statutory duties:

- A right to non-discrimination against disabled people in the field of employment. This includes a duty on employers to provide a 'reasonable adjustment' to working conditions or the working environment to overcome the practical effects of disability.
- A right to access to goods and services. This includes the removal of barriers and provision of aids, where reasonable.
- A right to redress against discrimination in occupational pension schemes and insurance services.
- A right to access to transport infrastructure, such as railways and bus stations, together with provisions which allow the Government to set minimum access criteria for new public transport vehicles (including buses, trains and taxis) to enable disabled people to use public transport more easily.
- A requirement that schools, colleges and universities provide information to disabled people about access to their facilities.
- The establishment of a National Disability Council to advise the government on issues and measures relating to the elimination of discrimination.

Criticisms of the law

The major criticism of the Disability Discrimination Act is that an important piece of civil rights legislation has been placed on the statute book without the provision of an effective means of enforcement. It is feared that the frequent references to 'reasonableness' will facilitate non-compliance by individuals and organisations, while at the same time making it difficult for those experiencing discrimination to prove their case. Furthermore there will be no powerful commission to oversee this important legislation. Although such commissions have been deemed necessary to monitor race relations and sexual discrimination legislation, the Conservative government had argued that the Disability Discrimination Act could be enforced and monitored satisfactorily by a quango with the status of an advisory body, the National Disability Council (NDC). The effectiveness of the legislation will also be supported by the courts and by the use of industrial tribunals in employment cases. The NDC is expected to consult with those it considers appropriate and pass on its proposals to the Secretary of State, who has the option of accepting the proposals in their entirety, making modifications, or rejecting them. If approved, the Secretary of State will submit a draft code to parliament. Either House may pass a resolution not to approve the draft, in which case 'the Secretary of State shall take no further steps in relation to the proposed code' (Disability Discrimination Act 1995, s42). The Secretary of State is also empowered to issue orders revoking codes of practice and 'may from time to time revise the whole or any part of the code and re-issue it' (Disability Discrimination Act 1995, s42).

The law has, in effect, established or reinforced two interrelated elements to what is termed and defined as disability:

- the physical, mental or sensory impairment of an individual;
- the social environment, artificial barriers and attitudes which prevent the individual from playing a full part in the life of the community.

Following from this, it can be seen how three types of discrimination against disabled people have been identified:

- direct discrimination, which means treating people less favourably than others because of their disability;
- indirect discrimination, which means imposing a requirement or condition on a job, facility or service which makes it harder for disabled people to gain access to it;
- unequal burdens, which means failing to take reasonable steps to remove barriers in the local environment that prevent disabled people participating equally.

The first two forms of discrimination are the same as those currently identified in the Disability Discrimination Act. They are also similar to the discriminations identified in the areas of race and gender legislation. In the case of direct and indirect discrimination an employer or service provider is committing an offence if they treat someone unfairly because they have an impairment. In the case of unequal burdens discrimination, the employer or service provider is committing an offence if they fail to adapt the environment to take account of an impaired person's incapacity when it would be reasonable for them so to do.

The concept of 'unequal burden' has nevertheless widened the definition of discrimination in relation to disabled people and is a distinguishing marker between disability discrimination and discrimination on racial and/or sexual grounds. The discrimination of 'unequal burden' 'exists when an artificial barrier, which could be removed by reasonable adaptation, prevents a disabled person from an opportunity enjoyed by a non -disabled person' (BCODP 1994).

Critics argue that the National Disability Council will be unrepresentative and not adequate for the task of enforcing the legislation. In addition it is envisaged that individuals will be forced to take private action, whereas in racial or sexual discrimination cases the relevant commissions can act on behalf of the aggrieved. The lack of corroborating evidence together with the cost of taking action may deter many people from seeking redress. Those dependent on state benefits, i.e. the majority of disabled people, are unlikely to have access to sufficient funds to pursue a claim, particularly since legal aid is unlikely to be available for such action. This concern was a major feature of debates before the Act became law. For the Liberal Democrats, Liz Lynne argued that it was a start but did not go far enough (*Guardian*, 29 March 1995). Alan Howarth (then a Conservative) warned that the lack of an enforcement body would leave 'a hole in the heart of this legislation', whilst Labour MP Tom Clarke argued that the legislation had 'no teeth'. William Hague, at that time the Government Minister for the Disabled, argued that setting up an enforcement body was bureaucratic and unnecessary, since the terms of the Act would provide for the assistance required by disabled people (*Guardian*, 28 March 1995). In effect, the United Kingdom would be the only country to have legislation to prevent discrimination against disabled people but no enforcement body (*Guardian*, 22 March 1995). Although the Disability Discrimination Act is less far-reaching than the Americans with Disabilities Act, it had been argued at the time of its passage through parliament that disabled people in Britain could find themselves with more rights than citizens of many European countries, so long as there are sufficiently powerful enforcement mechanisms. However, those seeking redress appear to be obliged to fight alone through the courts or industrial tribunals (*Guardian*, 28 March 1995) or be expected to meet the cost of such action from their own pockets no matter what the financial circumstances.

Tom Shakespeare is unequivocal in his condemnation of the Disability Discrimination Act. He argues that there is little merit in those who have been campaigning for the civil rights of disabled people settling for 'second-best' legislation. In his view, the prevalence of exemption clauses within the Act effectively announces that discrimination in some instances will be not only tolerated, but condoned. With its 'well-meaning messages promising inclusion and justice for disabled people' (*Guardian*, 30 March 1995), the Act guarantees nothing. Shakespeare is concerned that the UK Act is not only inferior to the Americans with Disabilities Act, but also falls short of Canadian and Australian measures. He took exception to William Hague's statement that Britain will lead the way in Europe with this legislation. On the contrary, says Shakespeare, 'Britain leads the field only in reluctance to support disabled citizens . . . and the pathetic substitute for civil rights legislation' (*Guardian*, 30

March 1995). According to Shakespeare, the United Kingdom lags behind Scandinavia, France, and Germany, where the constitution has been amended to prohibit discrimination against people with disabilities.

The provision of exemption clauses and qualifications within the wording of the Disability Discrimination Act weakens it substantially. Employers have a duty to modify their premises and working conditions, but regard will be paid to whether or not such modifications are 'practicable'. Thus, the financial cost to the employer of making changes can be taken into account, as can the employer's financial situation and 'the availability to the employer of financial or other assistance with respect to taking the step' (Disability Discrimination Act 1995, s5). In other words there are a range of circumstances under which employers have no obligation to change working practices and conditions that discriminate against disabled people.

Employers of fewer than 20 people are exempt from the legislation. With regard to transport, provision is made for licensing authorities to apply to the Secretary of State for exemption from some or all of the regulations relating to taxis and accessibility (s30). Similar exemption certificates may be issued in respect of rail vehicles. (s38). Although discrimination by providers of goods, facilities and services is outlawed, providers are only required to take 'reasonable' steps to change policies, practices or procedures that discriminate against disabled people (s18). Again there are a range of exemptions and circumstances in which discrimination is effectively 'justified'.

Caroline Gooding (1994, p. 98) issues a warning about using the courts to pursue claims. She suggests that the judiciary does not have a particularly high regard for the importance of discrimination as an issue:

> either in terms of individual rights or of the 'public interest'. The judiciary has tended to proceed on the basis that anti-discrimination legislation interferes with the freedom of individuals to discriminate, and the public interest is therefore best served by restricting the impact of that legislation to the maximum extent, thus implicitly valuing the freedom of discriminators above the rights of individuals to be free from discriminatory treatment.

If Gooding's is an accurate perception, disabled people's chances of redress are further diminished, and it becomes difficult to view the Act other than as an empty gesture which channels the needs of disabled people further down the road towards medically determined definitions that disregard the disabling effects of society.

The Disability Discrimination Act defines disability as: 'a physical or mental impairment which has a substantial and long term adverse effect on a person's ability to carry out normal day-to-day activities.' This definition has been challenged by disabled people and their organisations on a number of grounds:

- Does it really address protection against discrimination?
- Does it offer more opportunities for employment?
- Does it improve social and physical conditions for disabled people?

Who is protected?

The Act gives protection against discrimination to people who have or have had a disability which makes it 'substantially' difficult for them to carry out normal day-to-day activities. Only people who are (or who have been) 'disabled' under the Act's definition will be entitled to any of the new rights created by the Act.

- The disability can be physical or sensory, a learning disability or a mental health condition. It must be long-term (i.e. have lasted or be expected to last 12 months) or likely to recur.
- People with a history of disability are also protected, e.g. people who have recovered from mental illness, but continue to experience prejudice.
- People with a 'severe disfigurement' are deemed to be disabled.
- People with progressive conditions such as cancer, HIV infection or muscular dystrophy are protected provided their condition has, or has had, an impact (no matter how small) on their ability to carry out normal day-to-day activities.

There are particular cases and conditions that are included as disabling under the legislation. For example, severe disfigurement is treated as a disability even though this may have no effect on a person's ability to carry out day-to-day activities. However, disfigurement excludes tattoos and non-medical body piercing. People who are diagnosed as having progressive conditions such as cancer or HIV infection are covered from the time that their symptoms affect their ability to carry out day-to-day activities. For example, people who are HIV positive will only be protected from discrimination when they develop AIDS-related symptoms. The interpretation of day-to-day activity anticipates that it must include at least one of the following categories of behaviour:

- mobility – moving from place to place
- manual dexterity – e.g. use of the hands
- physical co-ordination
- continence
- the ability to lift, carry or move ordinary objects

- speech, hearing or eyesight
- memory, or the ability to concentrate, learn or understand
- being able to recognise physical danger.

It is, in effect, such a broad area that it is likely to be hard to define precisely. However, the concept of day-to-day activity is likely to be of particular concern to people with mental health problems or specific learning difficulties, who may be less able to claim discrimination under the Act than they can at present.

Opportunities for employment?

The Act prohibits discrimination against disabled people and seeks to prevent any significant disadvantage that a disabled person may encounter when applying for employment or when employed:

- The Act defines discrimination in the following terms: 'an Employer discriminates against a disabled person if for a reason which relates to the disabled person's disability he treats him less favourably than he treats or would treat others to whom that reason does not or would not apply, and he cannot show that the treatment is justified' (s5i.(a) and (b)).
- Less favourable treatment can only be legally justified if it is for a reason which is 'material to the circumstances of the particular case and substantial' (s5(4)).
- Employers have a duty to make 'reasonable' changes to the workplace or to the way in which work is done, where this is needed by a disabled employee or applicant.
- Trade unions and trade associations must not discriminate against disabled people in their provision of services and must make any reasonable adjustments which are required to make their services accessible.

It remains to be defined as to what is 'reasonable' in terms of making adjustments and when it is that discrimination can be legally 'justified'. As the Royal Association for Disability and Rehabilitation (RADAR) have pointed out, it is not yet clear how easy it will be for employers to justify unequal treatment. This will only become clear when case law is established. As has already been made clear, before an employer can use a person's disability as an excuse to overlook them, they will first have to consider whether a reasonable adjustment could solve the problem (e.g. if a person's job normally requires them to drive to visit customers and they are unable to drive because of their disability, an employer would have to consider whether other means of transportation would resolve the problem). In making a decision about what is 'reasonable' change in the workplace or working conditions, employers can take into account the cost of change balanced against their resources. For example, it might be considered reasonable to expect a large employer to install a lift at the workplace, but unreasonable for a smaller company or employer to make the same adjustments.

The Act does not apply to the police, the armed forces, prison officers and fire services. Neither does it apply to companies and organisations of fewer than 20 employees. This means that the quota system (whereby employers of more than 25 people had a duty to have 3 per cent of their work force as registered disabled people) has been abolished.

Improved social and physical conditions of disabled people?

While there was a strong lobby to ensure that the Disability Discrimination Act acknowledged the social model of disability, the final legislation contains numerous clauses that appear to steer towards the interests of the provider of services rather than recognising the discrimination experienced by disabled people. For instance, it will be unlawful to refuse to serve disabled customers in a restaurant, or provide them with a second-rate service, *unless this can be 'justified'*.

The Act indicates examples of situations where a provider of services can justify treatment which would otherwise be discriminatory:

- Where the treatment is necessary in order not to endanger the health or safety of any person (including the disabled person).
- Where the disabled person is incapable of giving informed consent or entering into an enforceable agreement and for that reason the treatment is reasonable in that case.
- Where refusal of treatment is necessary because the provider of services would otherwise be unable to provide the service to members of the public.

Policies, practices and procedures will have to be changed where reasonable, if they have the effect of discriminating against disabled people.

- Additional aids will have to be provided where this is reasonable given the size, resources and nature of the business (e.g. information on tape for blind customers).
- Physical barriers will have to be removed where this is reasonable and readily achievable.
- A reasonable adjustment will have to be made where it is impossible or unreasonably difficult for a disabled person to receive a comparable service to that which is provided for other people.
- As an alternative to removing barriers, goods or services may be provided by alternative means.

The goal is to ensure, as far as possible, that a service is provided at the same standard as that received by other people (e.g. access to a cinema). Whether the reality of this aspiration means that disabled cinema goers can sit wherever they wish appears to depend more on the ingenuity of individual cinema operators than on the legislation.

Enforcing the law

The Act has established a National Disability Council (NDC). This body will advise the government on how existing and new measures to help disabled people are working and recommend further changes where necessary.

National Disability Council

The NDC will only be able to advise the Secretary of State regarding strategies and will not be able to advise individuals or disability organisations. The Council will not advise on any matters relating to employment unless it is specifically asked to do so. The National Advisory Council on the Employment of Disabled People with Disabilities (NACEPD), which was established 50 years ago, will advise the government on the employment sections of the Act. The Act does, however, give the Secretary of State the power to abolish the older body (NACEPD), in which case the NDC will be expected to oversee all parts of the Act.

Ten of the seventeen members (59 per cent) appointed to the inaugural Council were disabled themselves or the parents or guardians of children with disabilities. However, it is disturbing to see that the NDC has no powers to investigate individual cases of discrimination. It has no powers to conduct formal enquiries in the manner of a commission such as the Commission for Racial Equality or the Equal Opportunities Commission. Without the powers and status of a commission the disability legislation continues to rely upon being monitored for 'reasonableness' as a way of countering discrimination against disabled people.

If a person with a disability feels that they have been discriminated against, they can instigate legal proceedings, and if successful they may be able to recover damages for any financial loss suffered, as well as damages for injuries to feelings. An instruction will also be issued that employers or service-providers should make a reasonable adjustment to provide access. The expectation is that individuals will have to seek advice and assistance through a solicitor, a Law Centre, trade union or Citizen's Advice Bureau.

In employment cases a complaint can be presented at an industrial tribunal; in the case of a complaint on the grounds of goods and services the local county court can be used. As by definition unemployment and under-employment are consistently higher among disabled people than their non-disabled contemporaries, it will be interesting to see how many disabled people can afford the costs of legal representation in such cases.

Employers are expected to think imaginatively and to acknowledge their responsibility towards disabled employees. It is evident that employment law is one way in which improvement can be realised in the circumstances of a range of disabled people. However, there are some warning signs on the horizon, emerging from the United States.

Provision in the United States

Both the United Kingdom and the United States are facing many of the same issues in relation to discrimination against people with disabilities. Whilst there is a growing awareness of the rights of people with disabilities in the USA, there is also a competing agenda for scarce resources from a population concerned with economic competition from the Pacific rim.

The United States has a population of approximately 264 million people, three quarters of whom live in towns or cities. Unlike Western Europe, the United States is experiencing a rapid growth in population. This is a consequence of the immigration boom since the mid-1960s, and especially since 1980. The new immigrants are primarily from Asia and Latin America; more than two million come from Mexico alone.

The United States has a federal democratic government. The Union comprises 50 states and each state has its own constitution. Local and state government deals with all matters not reserved for the federal government and the main unit of local government is the county. There are some 3,000 such counties in the 50 states. The national government has authority in matters such as general taxation, foreign affairs, federal and inter-state commerce, and crimes against the United States. It does not have a central role in relation to the social provision for disabled people provided by the individual states. Nevertheless, national government has passed a number of pieces of federal legislation that have had a direct impact on the interpretation of the new culture towards disabled people in each of the states of the Union.

The Americans with Disabilities Act

The Americans with Disabilities Act became law in 1990. Unlike the Disability Discrimination Act, the United States act is a civil rights statute and a much more comprehensive piece of legislation. It has become the model for disability legislation in Canada, Australia and New Zealand and was the foundation for the Civil Rights (Disabled Persons) Bill which was defeated on successive occasions in the United Kingdom parliament in 1991, 1992 and 1993.

The United States act was founded on the recognition that disability is a natural part of the human experience. Thus 'all citizens have an interest in ensuring that the values that form the basis of the Americans with Disabilities Act pervade our national life' (Burke 1995, p. 6). The values embodied in the Act – equal protection under the law, individual empowerment, freedom of association, economic opportunity – are important to and for all Americans. In passing the law, Congress stated the following facts concerning the life experiences of people with disabilities in America (see Burke 1995, p. 5):

- 43,000,000 Americans have one or more disabilities.
- National data indicate that individuals with disabilities occupy an inferior status in society and are severely disadvantaged socially, vocationally, economically and educationally.
- The continuing existence of unfair and unnecessary discrimination and prejudice denies people with disabilities the opportunity to compete on an equal basis and to pursue opportunities, costing the United States billions of dollars in unnecessary expenses resulting from dependency and non-productivity.

The Americans with Disabilities Act has been considered the 'most comprehensive federal civil rights law addressing discrimination against one fifth of the American population in all aspects of their daily lives. It is perhaps the most significant federal law since the Civil Rights Act of 1964' (Blanch 1994, p. 857).

Americans with physical or mental impairments that substantially limit daily activities are protected under the Act. These activities include working, walking, talking, seeing, hearing, or caring for oneself. People who have a record of such an impairment and those regarded as having an impairment are also protected. The Act has the following five titles or sections:

Title I   Employment
Title II   Public Services (including public transport)
Title III Public Accommodations and Services Operated by Private Entities

Title IV   Telecommunications
Title V   Miscellaneous Provisions

Title I Employment

This prohibits discrimination in employment against disabled people and requires employers to make reasonable accommodations to the known physical or mental limitations of a qualified applicant or employee, unless such accommodation would impose an undue hardship on the employer. Reasonable accommodations include such actions as making work sites accessible, modifying existing equipment, providing new devices, modifying work schedules and conditions, restructuring jobs and providing readers and interpreters.

Under the Act, employers with 15 or more employees must comply with the law. Title I also prohibits the use of employment tests and other selection criteria that screen out, or tend to screen out, individuals with disabilities, unless such tests or criteria are shown to be job-related. It also bans the use of pre-employment medical examinations or enquiries to determine if an applicant has a disability. The Act does, however, permit the use of medical examination after a job offer has been made, if the results are kept confidential. All people offered employment in the same job category are required to take these medical examinations and the results must not be used to discriminate.

Title II Public Services

This section requires that all the services and facilities associated with local and state government, as well as non-federal government agencies, are accessible to people with disabilities. In addition, Title II seeks to ensure that people with disabilities have access to transportation, e.g. all new buses must now be accessible. People who cannot use the standard public transportation facilities must be provided with an alternative supplementary para-transit service, unless this presents an undue burden.

In the area of rail transportation, the Act requires that all new rail vehicles and all new rail stations must become accessible within 20 years. Existing rail systems must have one accessible carriage per train. The network of subway, commuter, or underground trains must be made generally accessible.

Title III Public Accommodations

Public accommodations are interpreted as a broad range of services that include commercial sales, rental or service to the public. It includes educational institutions, recreational facilities and social service centres. The Act prohibits the use of criteria for establishing the right to use a service that may exclude or screen out people with disabilities (e.g. just as businesses hire a certain number of Spanish-speaking individuals to meet customer needs, they should be prepared to employ sign language interpreters).

It is anticipated that the Title III requirement for providing auxiliary aids will be interpreted flexibly. It is not expected to result in an undue burden being placed on business (e.g. a restaurant is not required to provide a menu in Braille if it is possible for the waiter to read out the menu). A business is entitled to choose among a range of alternatives for providing a service as long as the result is effective communication.

Existing public buildings should be made barrier-free wherever it is 'readily achievable' (i.e. when it can be accomplished easily and without too much expense). In most cases this includes ramping. However, new buildings (e.g. public and commercial office space and shops) must be made accessible to people with disabilities. Nevertheless, lifts are generally not required to be installed in buildings less than three stories high.

Title IV Telecommunications

Title IV requires that telephone companies provide effective telecommunication relay services. These must facilitate the communication of speech- or hearing-impaired individuals who use non-voice terminal devices. Such telecommunications systems also incorporate automatic teller machines at banks (ATMs) which will need to be made to 'talk'. There is a recognition of the need to develop rules governing the confidentiality of information resulting from assisted communication via message relay systems.

Title V Miscellaneous Provisions

This relates the Act to other laws such as the Rehabilitation Act of 1973, or the Hearing Aid Compatibility Act of 1988, which had required all new telephones to be made compatible with hearing aids; this section also relates to the provision of insurance.

A few longitudinal studies have addressed the effects of the Act on the lives of the people it was intended to benefit. Pfieffer (1996) has indicated that there is a divergence of opinion. Individual disabled people feel more empowered and see the law as a positive influence on attitudes, expectations and rights. Individuals in Pfieffer's survey also commented on improved physical accessibility which increased participation in the community: 'We expect things to be better and it makes us angrier when it's not. There is a real sense of "we're important" coming down' (Pfieffer 1996, p. 274).

This indication of individual liberation contrasts with some of the experiences of employers and bureaucrats operating at company and official state level in wider society. 'A personnel director said that they "have done almost nothing" and that if they "get sued they will probably do something"' (Pfieffer 1996, p. 274). A disabled activist also commented that:

> Most disabled people have no political savvy, no philosophical orientation so they eat up this shit and believe it until they find out that they're just as unemployed, getting in worse shape from the point of medical need, housing is not available to the mass of them, more and more of them are being found on the streets. (Pfieffer 1996, p. 276)

It is clear from people's experiences of the Act that individuals feel empowered and that they do not want to go back to the way things were (Pfieffer 1996; Burke 1996). However, it is also possible that the disability movement in the United States is becoming less radical and more complacent as the zeal of its early leaders fails to be replaced by younger, equally committed individuals (Johnstone 1996c).

There is a question about just how much this legislative change actually helps; particularly those who need help least, or those who need the most help. The argument is that affirmative action through legislation has gone too far (affirmative action is intended to establish preferences for minorities, e.g. black Americans, whereby preferential recruitment is given in favour of black students on American college campuses). It was well grounded as a morally defensible goal for aggrieved minorities such as black Americans claiming reparations against white American domination, 'but somewhere over the years, it changed from reparations policy to diversity policy, including not only blacks but women, Latinos and all minority groups' (Tomasky 1996). This stretching of diversity across oppressed constituencies has not been sustained through the weight of public opinion but by court orders and codes of practice. At a time when everyone is faced with job uncertainty, declining living standards and reduced wages, it arguably becomes harder to justify the support for affirmative action for all minorities and under-represented groups. It is in this universal climate and under such a shift in circumstances that legislative change and equal opportunities for disabled people is emerging in the United Kingdom. However, it is arguable whether affirmative action towards disabled people in the United Kingdom has the same historical and moral claim to make as that which seeks to atone for the particularly horrid history of white treatment of blacks in the USA.

The re-emergence of segregation

In the United States there is a strong recent history of tackling discrimination through legislation and through affirmative action. The Civil Rights marches of the 1950s and 1960s led to legislation that challenged racially segregated education and employment practices. These actions influenced the emergence of equal opportunities legislation for disabled people. However, the 1990s has seen the beginnings of a rejection of affirmative action in the United States. Any affirmative action for disabled people could be subject to the same reversals. This has begun to be particularly noticeable in the area of services in community colleges and local communities in the USA where resources for learning support have begun to be closely scrutinised and cut back (Cooper 1996; O'Day 1996).

In the United Kingdom the limitations of the Disability Discrimination Act are acknowledged by the majority of disability organisations. There is a real probability that disabled people, who cannot participate effectively in the democratic process and whose needs involve additional expenditure in the workplace, will continue to face the prospect of being singled out for 'special treatment'. National disability groups are growing increasingly insistent that comprehensive civil rights for disabled people have not been achieved. The Act does not give disabled people rights and they are still considered second-class citizens with second class rights and opportunities. Discrimination in the electoral process begins at the polling stations. It has been estimated that only 12 per cent of polling stations are fully accessible (Disability Now 1996); and that although people with learning difficulties are entitled to vote, the problem is that hardly any do. Research by MENCAP shows that only 5 per cent of people with learning difficulties used their vote in the 1992 General Election (see Hirst 1996, p. 23).

Summary

Both the Disability Discrimination Act in the United Kingdom and the Americans with Disabilities Act in the USA have defined and established disability issues within equal opportunities legislation. Both acts encourage disabled people to use litigation as a method for ensuring employment opportunities, access to goods and services, access to public buildings and access to public transport. However, whereas the Americans with Disabilities Act has been perceived as a way of empowering disabled people within the wider context of civil rights, the Disability Discrimination Act has been viewed by disabled people as a somewhat piecemeal and negative response to civil rights in the UK. The political response of disabled people to the Disability Discrimination Act is examined in Chapter 6. There was anticipation that the Act would go some way to improve the 'quality of life' of people with disabilities and this issue is investigated in the next chapter.

CHAPTER 4

What is quality of life?

Questions

- What do you understand by 'quality of life' and what are its components?
- What does quality of life mean within the context of a market economy?
- The issue of quality is relative. Simple choices are not problematic. What are some of the more complex measures of quality in terms of disability discrimination?
- What do you consider advocacy to be in relation to empowerment and the widening of choice for disabled people?

Introduction

This chapter sets out to explore one of the key issues that lies at the heart of Disability Studies. 'Quality of life' has been defined as 'an overall general well-being that is comprised of objective and subjective evaluations of physical, material, social and emotional well-being together with the extent of personal development and purposeful activity, all weighted by a personal set of values' (Felce and Perry 1996, p. 52). And such a definition is consistent with an explanation that recognises quality of life as a multi-dimensional construct. A three-element conceptualisation of quality of life, containing five domains of well-being, is reproduced as Figure 4.1. A model such as this also forces us to focus upon stereotypical representations of lifestyles: an issue that is particularly pertinent to disabled people and the manner in which images of disability are perpetuated in our culture. In any event the concept of quality in daily living forces us to consider the interrelationship between objective measures (such as health, income, housing quality, friendship networks, activity and social roles), and more loosely defined and subjective markers. These refer to constructs such as personal satisfaction with life circumstances and the rating of the feeling of well-being in a range of different life conditions, e.g. judgement of personal accomplishment at different stages of the life cycle.

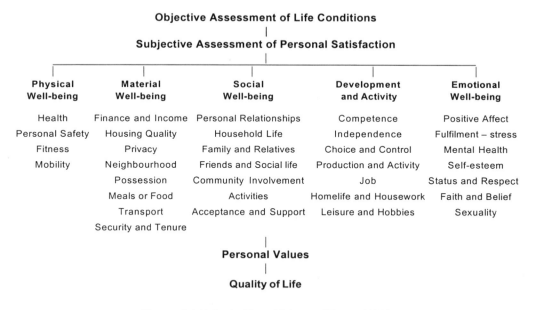

Figure 4.1 (Adapted from Felce and Perry 1996)

Many of the markers of 'quality of life' are clearly subjective and personalised perceptions of one's place in the environment and the responses that one receives from others. Brown *et al.* (1992), reporting on research conducted in Canada, have addressed the complexity of the term, indicating that quality of life is not simply about happiness and satisfaction, but also about striving and dissatisfaction. A similar attempt to measure quality of life indicators has been attempted in Europe (Moniga and Vianello 1995). The range of discourses suggest that there are fundamental implications for both service-providers, carers and the opinions of disabled people. Research suggests that 'quality of life' is a complex concept not only represented by balances between satisfaction and dissatisfaction; primarily it is about gaining a positive self-image and a sense of empowerment and control over the mechanisms that regulate one's environment.

Quality of life: an eternal paradox?

Johnstone (1995) has indicated, with reference to the United Kingdom, and Banfelvy (1996) in a wider European context, that there is a looming crisis of confidence around the concept of quality of life in general. There are those who claim that welfare has eroded the work ethic and the moral fibre of a nation's workforce (Herrnstein and Murray 1994). As we approach the end of the century, new conditions are being imposed on benefits, and tough law and order measures introduced in order to control antisocial behaviour. This millennial tension is being echoed in the search for moral guidance in our leaders and our public services. The apparent failure of human relations has also disadvantaged many people who are perceived to be socially as well as sensorily, cognitively, or physically disabled. Disabled people lead lives in which they will have been treated ambivalently. This often manifests itself in a kind of social inappropriateness, where disabled people perceive themselves not only as different, but also as unprepared, or unwilling to adjust to all social situations. This can result in the repression of effective relationships in the home, community and the workplace.

The inability to fulfil the expectations of those around you, or the hopes of significant others, is a large burden, and reactions can take the form of withdrawal and depression. At the same time there is often a disappointing lack of contact between disabled people themselves. There are few opportunities to establish and maintain intimate and mutually respectful friendships in settings that are constantly supervised. In such circumstances and with such fragile relationships, many disabled people do really need more contact with trusted companions who are capable of forming a social 'umbrella' of support to encourage them to form wider social networks and friendships. Such a network can cross the boundaries of generations, social status and gender.

Finance, or the lack of it, has already been indicated as a source of real hardship to all people without qualifications. The wage earned in low-paid open employment is little different from the amount paid to people on training programmes or receiving social security payments. For many people with disabilities, some of whom may be entitled to higher allowances due to disability, their welfare entitlements can far exceed their realistic earning potential. A failure of citizenship on the part of the whole society forces many disabled people to remain financially disadvantaged by a range of circumstances. Independence for them becomes an illusion. Either they remain living at home with their families, or they become economically dependent upon others; perhaps in the form of a spouse, partner or the state. If disabled people try to live alone or to join groups they can rapidly run into financial difficulties and confrontations with bureaucratic regulations. In such circumstances, where the bureaucratic procedures of an independent adult status are only beginning to be understood, it is important to be able to turn to somebody for knowledgeable advice.

Those who are unfamiliar with handling the requirements of increasing bureaucracy may try to avoid contact with official authority, be it an institution or an agency. Quality of life may begin with the need for help in getting hold of such things as birth certificates, identity cards, passports, registration certificates. There may be need for advice on how to obtain insurances and how to cancel the same if they are inadequate or too expensive. There may be need for technical support in dealing with public correspondence; for example, in response to notices or demands, or how to appeal against procedural decisions that may affect their lives. The ability to respond effectively can be a key factor in raising an individual's level of self-confidence and feelings of self-esteem.

Quality of life as an array of variables

The model of quality of life indicated in Figure 4.1 has tended to be founded on the lifestyles of non-disabled people and the normal social rhythms and circumstances that are so frequently considered as fundamental. As such it is an atheoretical, simple rights-based model similar to the work of O'Brien's 'Five Accomplishments' (O'Brien and Tyne 1981). Research studies in the UK and Europe (e.g. Moniga and Vianello 1995; Berrington *et al.* 1996) investigating quality of life measures identified by disabled people suggest that the concept can be considered as a product of a number of interconnected variables. Thus, the construct of 'quality of life' can be organised by both subjective and objective criteria.

- *Material well-being.* This is a potentially sensitive area. As well as income levels, it might include observations and judgements about matters such as the quality of housing, lifetime changes in relation to residence, financial circumstances, transport availability.
- *Physical well-being.* This includes any additional impairments, the need to use adaptations or prosthetic equipment. It might involve understanding of specialist services, e.g. speech therapy, chiropody, dieticians. Certainly it will incorporate an awareness of the importance of health and fitness, exercise and safety.
- *Social well-being.* This suggests community involvement as well as personal relationships. It will involve an understanding of the sources of support, aspects of everyday living and sources of help and advice in the community.
- *Development and activity.* While linked to objective measures of employment, this variable is also to do with subjectively perceived levels of independence and the opportunities for choice and control in people's

lives. It may refer to opportunities for education and training, including the uses made of day centres.

- *Emotional well-being.* This is tied to feelings of self-worth; the levels of status and respect accorded to and subjectively assumed by people. It is also linked with the sense of fulfilment that people attach to their lives.
- *Mobility.* In order to properly develop quality of life, the mobility of disabled people has to be addressed and promoted. The awareness and removal of a number of architectural barriers (stairs and entrances to houses, toilets and public buildings) has improved across the United Kingdom and throughout Europe as a result of legislation. These, together with adaptations to the means of transport (buses, trains, aeroplanes, taxis) and improvement in signage and the provision of information (sonorous traffic lights, tactile signs), are fundamental considerations for any adequate measures of effective quality of life.
- *Housing/dwelling place.* There are many different considerations that must be taken into account when the housing needs of disabled people are considered. On one side of the argument there are all the difficulties related to the level of autonomy of the person; on the other there are the real practical considerations of people with physical and sensory impairments. We have also to distinguish between the perceived needs of those who continue to live in an institution and those in a group home, or those who share a house or apartment and those who live and dwell independently.
- *Leisure time.* Quality of life is not only determined by the health and employment prospects of an individual, but also by opportunities that come together during leisure time. Holiday resorts, holiday houses, camping, recreational and sporting facilities must all be considered and made suitably accessible and available. There is a tendency for marked differentiations in this area. For example, in sport, on the one hand there are some activities designated only for disabled athletes and disabled sports people, while alternatively, it is considered by others that sport and recreation is an ideal medium for promoting inclusion in community settings.
- *Vocational training.* Many people with disabilities are invisible to the general public following years of segregated educational provision. The majority of disabled school-leavers, it is argued, do not have the prerequisite skills for employment and this identifies them as having special training needs, regardless of whether this was evident whilst they were at school. These notions echo Freeman (1988) who has argued that disabled and 'delinquent' young people leaving school have been crudely redefined as not only unskilled but also socially incompetent and in need of

categorical programmes of vocational training and further training in social skills.

A great variety of vocational programmes for disabled people have been established across Europe. They are based on the principles of developing successful and satisfying placements in both the work place and wider society. The programmes tend towards specific skills training, but also teach the social behaviours and habits that are usually considered desirable in a work setting. Education and training in basic skills is also maintained; with an emphasis on concepts such as self-advocacy, independence, self-determination and citizenship. It is evident that vocational training is emerging as an extension of the inclusive educational principles that are in favour in schools. It follows that vocational training which favours self-determination and independence also stresses the importance of changing attitudes towards disabled people. Perhaps this requires a re-negotiation of the relationships between young people, their parents, teachers and social workers.

- *Access to work/employment.* In traditional, industrial society terms, the theory of a person's value within the workplace has been argued something like this: employment potential is determined by an employee's efficiency and productivity and those people who are not capable of benefiting from training are not likely to be either economically efficient or profitable. By definition, it is argued, disabled people are less capable and more dependent than non-disabled people; therefore they are both at a disadvantage and more expensive. These attitudinal barriers are deeply rooted and whilst special training initiatives have expanded for all young people they have also helped to provide a new justification for the subtle perpetuation of prejudices that limit the social and economic position of an increasing number of disillusioned and alienated young people. At the same time, work opportunities for disabled people are in danger of being redefined in order to include a growing population of those described as the underclass – people who are socially and economically deprived, rather than disadvantaged through impairments. As jobs have disappeared and special services have been redefined in order to incorporate this underclass, we are beginning to see the expansion of special provision for those deemed as failures economically and vocationally. Whether this has arisen as a result of deliberate strategies by successive governments rather than through the actions of individuals is worth some consideration.

Until recently there have really been only three alternatives for the employment of disabled and handicapped people: normal placement in a working place with some adaptations; employment in a sheltered facility, or unemployment with the possibility of therapeutic earnings. Recent legislative changes, in relation to disability discrimination particularly in the United Kingdom and North America, have influenced some changes in the working opportunities of people with sensory and physical impairments. However, the legislation will only apply to companies that employ more than 20 people and is, thereby, of little consequence to some 96 per cent of employers.

The deliberate denial of quality of life

The emergence of the disability movement in the United Kingdom is integral to the understanding of 'quality of life'. The exercise of choice and the opportunity to take control of the organisation of one's own life is one of the first markers of quality. It is significant that for many people with disabilities this is still an aspiration rather than a reality. Campbell and Oliver (1996) have assembled an eloquent testimony to the many disabled people who have been, and are still, involved in raising awareness of the exclusion of disabled people in society. Quality of life is a human rights issue.

In industrial economies with relatively sophisticated and affluent political and economic systems, an infrastructure of professional services has been built to provide extensive support designed to enhance the quality of life of disabled people. The decision to compensate individuals for loss of income arising from disability, through the payment of lump-sum benefits, is a case in point. Other examples of improved quality of life could include subsidised, adapted housing and transport services. Specialist services have begun to be developed as groups of people with specific conditions have formed themselves into powerful organisations to promote the interests of self-recognised groups with 'disease-specific' disablements, e.g. asthma, allergies, arthritis, dyslexia.

The physical health of young people with disabilities is often a factor in the accumulation of multiple disadvantage. Poor hygiene and poverty are not automatic correlates with disability but they clearly affect levels of physical and psychological self-confidence. Whilst at school, physical development and patterns of health can be observed and monitored as part of the curriculum and school life. If necessary, medical services and treatment can be arranged. The government targets for improving health and fitness set out in *The Health of the Nation* (HMSO 1992) have included a suggestion for more 'competitive' games for people with disabilities. These may not usefully relate to the promotion of health, but they do at least recognise the place of activity in physical growth as an aspect of quality of life.

The promotion of health and sport during school years is unavailable outside the formal years of education. There is no mandatory requirement nor a prescribed curriculum in sports and health in further education colleges and neither is there any medical monitoring. The opportunities for organised sport for disabled people may be reduced as individuals are left to their own devices. However, it is now widely acknowledged that lots of non-competitive activities, e.g. dance, yoga, aerobics, swimming, are ultimately better for the development of health than organised team games. These might be better considered in discussions about measures of quality of life for all people, but particularly those with disabilities.

It is clear from the above that many people with disabilities can become multiply disadvantaged by a lack of basic care in the areas such as personal hygiene, laundry and sometimes reasonable nourishment. If one lacks basic amenities and has only a temporary address, one is immediately disadvantaged in terms of employment. 'No dwelling, no job' is a basic rule for all people of lower status in society and this includes many people with disabilities.

Successful living in a community is fraught with prejudice and economic inequalities. The 'community' can itself be highly oppressive and unjust. As this text has already indicated, at certain stages in history communities have demonstrated extremes of intolerance towards minorities. Gould (1996) outlines and chronicles how systems of control are frequently predicated on deliberate prejudice and have been used to oppress a range of minorities. We need to recognise that the community itself can be a force for oppression, exhibiting a level of intolerance that continues in society to the present day.

As has been noted by many writers (e.g. Corbett and Barton 1992; Johnstone 1995), empowerment can only come about if the powerful are prepared to relinquish power. The isolated experiences of the majority of disabled people mean that it is unrealistic to expect that they will set out to claim power. As we are reminded, this in itself becomes its own form of oppression. There is a considerable issue here, that challenges the purpose of what constitutes 'real help'. As the numbers of self-help groups and support networks increase, there is a growing and visible solidarity amongst a range of minority groups, including disabled people. This inevitably challenges the role and function of the 'professional.' However, as we have seen, professionals are often involved in the setting up and maintenance of self-advocacy groups and they have to face up to the often disturbing realisation that their involvement sustains the oppression that the groups are intended to overcome. The repercussions of real choice and effective empowerment mean that there will be some inevitable conflicts. This involves professionals and parents having to readjust to a range of new and often uncomfortable realities.

The argument that empowerment lies at the heart of 'quality of life' is a mark of a mature society. In supporting empowerment, professionals have to shift their practices and also their mindset – moving beyond tokenism and 'fix it quick' solutions. All too often the status quo is maintained under the guise of innovation; 'speaking for yourselves' is confined to curricular programmes and simulations in classrooms:

> To challenge it involves a fundamental and courageous shift of roles. Only through this creative process will new and innovative identities be forged. If tolerance is to be fostered, this will help define the parameters of what constitutes 'successful' living. (Corbett and Barton 1992, p. 76)

Successful living and quality of life leads us back to the consideration of the deeper set of values that underpin the exploration of liberation. As Coleridge (1993) has pointed out, basic needs are lacks which need to be supplied – like food, shelter and health. However, there is a clear problem if the development of quality of life is restricted to the process of meeting needs in this way. At the heart of the problem lies the fact that such needs are passive. Quality of life needs are also active.

There are other needs which are just as basic. There is 'the need to be creative, to make choices, to exercise judgement, to love others, to have friendships, to contribute something of oneself to the world, to have social function and purpose' (Coleridge 1993, p. 52). If these needs are not met the result is the impoverishment of the human spirit. In Coleridge's view any enquiry into disability, and the social and political forces that surround the concept, brings us all face-to-face with the purposes of survival, the way justice does or does not happen and the central question of human relationships. The areas of life that contribute to 'quality' are ultimately the same for us all. They apply to everybody. We cannot use the argument that they apply to some and not to others. We certainly cannot say that it only applies to that portion of the population that is classified as disabled:

> We can start by accepting that disability exists. It is part of human life, part of the way things are. Let us engage with it, enquire into it, make friends with it. Disabled people do it from the inside, people who are not yet disabled need to do it from the outside. (Coleridge 1993, p. 216)

The community base in the development of quality of life

Quality of life in any country has to take account of the ecological, socio-economic and cultural characteristics of the geographic area concerned. This principle lies at the heart of the move towards inclusive community provision and away from institutional rehabilitation with its centralised, capital-intensive emphasis on normalisation.

With few exceptions, established community groups and charities still see disability as basically a medical problem. Nevertheless, some housing associations in the UK have started to construct accessible houses and apartments, using the Scandinavian 'Fokus' system as a model. Charitable organisations like the Community Service Volunteers (CSV) have established community-based support systems. However, there is an important difference between their approach and that of the movement of disabled people campaigning for disability rights: 'Local Authorities, Health Authorities and charities tend not to see independent living as a basic human right as we do. For them independent living is still a welfare issue' (Bracking 1993).

Community-based rehabilitation

It was in a serious attempt to deinstitutionalise, demystify and deprofessionalise rehabilitation that the concept of community-based rehabilitation (CBR) was born. At its heart it shares much in common with other philosophies that are humanistic and aimed at promoting personal dignity. The term has, nevertheless, been widely misapplied and CBR is still a generally misunderstood process. CBR sets out to promote awareness and responsibility for rehabilitation within local communities; it deliberately targets self-reliance. Disabled people, their families and all members of the community are expected to take an active part in the process of building their own common solutions.

The premise of CBR is deceptively simple: a local supervisor is recruited from the community and receives training; the supervisor then trains the immediate and extended family of the disabled person in basic rehabilitation skills, the extended family being, in turn, supported by the community. Quality of life within a CBR programme is thus based on two rather old-fashioned assumptions:

- that the greatest resource for helping a disabled person is his or her own family;
- that the community around the family can be mobilised for the development of support.

The role of the family is fundamental for building relationships and social development in most societies. However, its relationship to the rehabilitation of disabled people in the community is more problematic. The family has always been one of the main sources of learning support and help to a disabled child. But the quality of this provision varies and is not always guaranteed, e.g. there may be emotional or practical factors that prevent a family from helping in all circumstances. At a practical level, there may be simply not enough time or money to provide an adequate amount of rehabilitation for an individual. This need not imply a lack of care, but is an illustration of the fact that absolute poverty concentrates the mind to focus on the absolute essentials of life. As Coleridge (1993, p. 86) reminds us, 'As soon as services become available, parents will use them for their children, but they may not have the energy or time to do systematic rehabilitation themselves.'

At the emotional, more affective level, the function of the parent is different from the role carried out by the paid professional therapist or counsellor. The relationship between parent and child carries a set of emotions that do not exist between the child and a therapist operating outside the family. The birth of a disabled child may have produced an undercurrent of guilt in the parents, and led to the often described cycle of over-protection and under-expectation associated with parenting a disabled child. Over-protection, rather than neglect, is more frequently a cause of underachievement in people with disabilities.

The other important feature of CBR is the involvement of the community in action. However, it is extremely difficult to impose a community approach by government decree, in a hierarchy of authority, from the top. The concept of 'community' is certainly an organic one which grows and changes. But an effective community is not a collection of bland assumptions that build on the belief that everyone is prepared to work together harmoniously. Families, neighbours, health services, social workers, local authorities, employers, carpenters, etc. all play their part in meeting the needs of disabled people. But the subtle dynamics of communities will always need to be considered and development workers should tap into existing community patterns and interests rather than attempt to set up projects that may result in the destruction of existing community strengths.

The development of community-based rehabilitation

CBR was originally developed to meet the needs of communities in isolation from generic medical and educational services (Thorburn and Marfo 1990). It has been particularly applicable to remediation and rehabilitation programmes that address childhood disability in developing countries and to people in rural economies (e.g. those engaged in agriculture, farming, fishing). The World Health Organisation (WHO) and UNESCO/UNICEF have established numerous functional, 'basic needs' and community-based rehabilitation programmes. These programmes have addressed instruction and training in the non-formal and more functional areas of selection and maintenance of safe water supplies; methods of waste disposal; growing, storing and consumption of more and better quality foods and nutritional education.

CBR is centred around generic 'home-grown' interventions and can be traced back to the activities of the World Health Organisation in 1976 (WHO 1982). By the early 1980s, WHO was claiming that CBR was 'an appropriate, effective, feasible and economically viable approach to provide the most essential rehabilitation to the disabled persons not now reached by services in the developing countries. CBR should form part of the primary health care programme' (WHO 1982, p. 19).

CBR is designed as a three-tiered model of comprehensive rehabilitation intended to build on the resources of the community. The model has been commented upon by many authors (e.g. Miles 1981, 1990; Kalyanpur 1996).

The first level of basic community provision comprises disabled people and consumers (the consumers being disabled people's families and community workers, together with existing community agencies both statutory and voluntary). A community health worker, called the local supervisor, is recruited and trained in the application of simple and basic rehabilitation techniques using the CBR Training Manual (Helander *et al.* 1983). The local supervisor identifies the individual with disabilities, assesses the severity of the condition and then trains a member of the individual's family to provide ongoing rehabilitation. More sophisticated and professional rehabilitation would require referrals to the next two levels of specialisation. The second or intermediate support level involves existing general health services with staff that have a higher level of competence and more sophisticated resources than those found at the community level. Since services at this level are not disability-specific, personnel such as physicians, nurses, teachers, midwives and social workers will be required to receive training in the areas of disability prevention and rehabilitation. The third and final specialised service level consists of speciality areas, including medical, vocational rehabilitation, special education and social services. The quality and quantity of these rehabilitation services varies throughout almost all developing countries.

CBR projects have been commended for their pioneering efforts to involve community and family members. The techniques have also been praised for their emphasis on functional rather than clinical treatments. However, critics have argued for revision of an underlying philosophy that assumes a predetermined inclination towards people with disabilities where, in fact, none exists (Miles 1996).

Werner (1987) states that the model assumes a considerably sophisticated level of coordination of health, vocational, educational and social services in countries and regions where disability issues are a low priority. This point is illustrated by early evaluations of CBR in India (Ephraem 1984; Hariharan

1982). Attempts to incorporate CBR within the rubric of primary health care services soon began to meet with opposition from village health workers. Despite monetary incentives, the community health workers resented the additional responsibilities and complained of work overload. According to Hariharan, traditional prejudice against disabled people accounted for the reluctance among the local supervisors to provide rehabilitation services.

Further criticism of CBR has centred on the three-tiered process of implementation. Far from empowering people, it is claimed that the system prevents people from gaining access to information and resources (Miles 1985, 1990; O'Toole 1987). In his review of CBR across developing countries, Miles (1985) has stated that as parents become increasingly dependent upon the local supervisor for technical advice they cease to use their own creative resources to develop alternatives. In addition the responsibility for caring for the disabled person falls exclusively upon the immediate and extended family. Circumstances such as this beg the question of the meaning of community responsibility. In reality the process develops into little more than the mobilisation of people's resources subsidising government-controlled programmes. Miles (1981) had been amongst the first to note that CBR tends to impose a top-down approach that is entirely inappropriate for some parts of the world:

> The concept of individual 'self-fulfilment, stressing one's "maximum potential" being "normalised" and "integrated into society"' are part of a Western package of ideals and philosophy . . . . The value inequality of human beings, by reason of birth, caste, skin pigmentation, economic and social status, is a fundamental tenet throughout Asia, whereas the educated Westerner tends to cherish an ideal of value-equality, while being highly competitive, individualistic and intolerant of under-achievement. (Miles 1981, p. 7)

Threats to quality of life

No systematic studies have yet been carried out to assess the extent to which warfare and violence contribute to disability. Where impairments arise as a consequence of violence, this in turn can lead to social abandonment and disablement (e.g. the physical impairments arising from the estimated thousands of amputations on soldiers and civilians surviving the conflicts in former Yugoslavia, Vietnam and Northern Ireland). Similar deliberate atrocities have resulted as a consequence of abandoned booby trap land-mines and have been reported by Save the Children in Afghanistan, Mozambique and other parts of the world. In Cambodia it is estimated there are some 7 to 10 million land-mines abandoned from civil conflicts and that they continue to injure and maim some 60 to 70 people a month (Barron, 'The Mine Clearers', BBC Radio 4, 6 November 1996). However, the associated trauma of mental health complications resulting from such violence is the much more common experience of victims, rather than physical disablement. Severe psychiatric diseases or disturbances are seen among many who have either participated in, or lived through, war. Violence can escalate the motive for revenge and lead to murder, attempted murder, armed fights with guns, knives and other weapons (Helander 1993, p. 28).

Family conflicts, when combined with alcohol and drug abuse, may mean that women are particularly at risk of being battered by their husbands or partners. Incest and rape have been noted as the commonest causes of pregnancy amongst girls aged 12 to 16 in the maternity wards of some South American cities (Heise 1992). Though under-diagnosed and hidden, the abuse of people with disabilities is frequent and there is a high incidence affecting people with learning difficulties. A study by UNICEF from Somalia, covering four district hospitals each serving about 100,000 people, indicated that:

> it was surprising to find that in the hospital records dating two years back, the only patients admitted for treatment in the hospital consisted of hundreds of cases listed as 'wounds'. The hospital staff described these 'wounds' as resulting from domestic violence and other forms of community fighting. (Helander 1993, p. 28)

Disability and quality of life in developing countries

Historically, provision for people with disabilities has been ignored in developing countries where the economic and material basis for living tends to be impoverished. There has been an absence of suitable textbooks describing the circumstances and needs of people with disabilities in the developing world. Those that have been available are usually adopted from a Western European cultural perspective. Any detailed discussion that does emerge is frequently based on generalisations that are assumed to be held in common, but, in reality, are of relatively minor importance. Baine (1988) and Kalyanpur (1996) both suggest that this has served to diminish discussion around those issues of major concern and real community needs. For example, the tests and methods of special education recommended for use in Western countries are quite inappropriate for use in developing countries. Any tests developed with Western children will usually be culturally biased; materials, specialised personnel and physical facilities recommended and anticipated in the classrooms of Europe are simply not available in developing countries. Presupposed considerations about the quality of life of disabled people developed in England, Europe and America have little relationship with the day-to-day circumstances of the countries to which they have been exported.

Our consideration of quality of life has so far indicated how both a business ethos and the ideology of the market place have influenced and defined the understanding of disability in both capitalist and centralised economies. The new rationale for the provision of services in developing countries is to give a more fundamental meaning to the concept of quality of life as liberation. This includes equal access to educational opportunities for all learners, regardless of their physical, emotional and intellectual impairments. However, these objectives cannot be achieved without an adequate understanding of the wider political marginalisation of disabled people. Nkabinde (1993), writing with reference to the emerging political order in the new South Africa, has suggested that there is a rising number of young people with disabilities at risk due to political violence, neglect, torture and abuse. This is only one reason why services, including health education, and an understanding of the social model of disability can play a great role in changing social conditions and the quality of life.

In developing countries, as everywhere else, cultures and belief systems tend to spring from the basic premise that the community is a hierarchically ordered unit that is superior to the individual. In India, for example, independence and 'quality of life' are defined very differently from Western conceptions:

> In the West the child is encouraged to 'grow up', to 'be a big boy', to do things for himself, and he is praised for taking such initiatives. The situation is quite the contrary in India . . . . I have seen boys of five and six years of age sitting quietly while mother or servant or relative feeds them . . . . The situation is similar with the processes of bathing and dressing. This is a factor to be considered in the care of the handicapped child, in light of our desire to make him as independent and 'normal' as possible. (Nimbkar 1971, p. 8)

This emergence of disability awareness in the developing world runs in uncomfortable parallel with the examination of disability as a legitimate area of study in general. Any discussion that emerges cannot, however, avoid exposure to many of the underlying prejudices of racial segregation and the uncaring treatment of many black and Asian people with disabilities.

From rehabilitation to self-advocacy – 'nothing about me, without me'

There are a variety of considerations of the term advocacy. Amongst the most common are:

- *Legal advocacy*, which usually refers to lawyers helping people exercise or defend their legal rights, but can also include people like Welfare Rights Services assisting people with benefit entitlements and representing people at Benefits Appeals.
- *Group advocacy*, which refers to people uniting to campaign on issues affecting a particular group or cause. It is particularly associated with the function and role of pressure groups.
- *Citizen advocacy*, which involves partnership between a vulnerable person and a member of the public on a long-term basis, in order to establish and protect the person's long-term interests.
- *Self-advocacy:* which often means individuals exercising their skills, to express their views on their own behalf. Sometimes self-advocacy involves people coming together through self-directed peer groups. This encourages and enables members to gather the confidence to speak up for themselves. Good examples of this development would be the development of self-advocacy groups by people with learning difficulties creating the People First Movement, or in the mental health field, Survivors Speak Out.

If we recognise how the inequality of people with disabilities has been constructed and continues to provide a basis for a social policy of exclusion, where does this leave the concept of quality of life in relation to self-advocacy? The inequalities inherent in the social structure of our institutions have been touched upon in this chapter, but the emphasis has been on the state. The development of services and the subject matter of instruction has tended to ignore the daily life experience of people with disabilities. What is required is a shift towards a new framework for measuring the quality of life and a redefinition of the so-called problems of disability. Rather than seeing the problem as something rooted in people with disabilities, it needs to be recognised as a feature of the inequality that is inherent in the social and economic structure of society. Rioux (1996) encapsulates this point:

> If we wish to work towards societies that are distinguished by a culture of justice and the public ownership of private disadvantage, we have to find a framework that takes into account and makes policy that includes all people, including those who do not fit conventional norms. This deconstruction of inequality will have to be addressed by concerted coherent action. (Rioux 1996, p. 131)

Self-advocacy is a fashionable term for an old concept which is integral to any understanding of 'quality of life'. It is about seeking and gaining additional information about rights, responsibilities and entitlements for oneself or a group. Trades unions provide a good example of group advocacy; offering people who feel marginalised the infrastructure and opportunity to come together to gain strength through a collective voice. Self-advocacy, therefore, continues the act of making choices and decisions and bringing about desired change for oneself. Crawley (1988, 1989) has suggested that any activity that involves self-determination, or people asserting themselves rather than having their interests advanced by others, can be called self-advocacy. This means that it can range from very simple things such as indicating whether or not you like the food you are given, to more complex actions such as choosing whether or not to go on strike for higher wages.

Both advocacy and self-advocacy are, thus, on the same continuum but at opposite ends of the scale. The need for advocacy stems from the difficulties that we all face in modern societies from time to time. It is a truism that all individuals feel marginalised at certain times and somebody speaking on our behalf can help to facilitate change. The relative distribution of power in society means that some individuals are not always in a position to represent their own interests. This can arise as a result of intolerance, prejudice and fear. It can be due to the restrictions imposed by an individual impairment or due to the disabling or restricting environment in which someone lives. People without the means of access to power, or organisations in which their views can be heard or listened to, are doubly disadvantaged. For example, those who are deemed too old, too disabled, too poor, or somehow too far beyond the pale of society's cultural norms, are diminished in terms of their citizenship. Advocacy is a tool for challenging this disempowerment and attempting to re-establish people's sense of self-respect, dignity and self-confidence. It can be conducted on a personal or a group basis. But, above all else, it is about getting your voice heard.

The principles of all advocacy work are founded on respect, dignity and empowerment. This is particularly the case in relation to people with disabilities. As far as possible, advocates work to support individuals to help themselves and to ensure that the advocate does nothing to further disempower the individual by taking control or imposing their own agenda.

Within a social policy context, the need for effective advocacy for disabled people was officially first recognised in 1986. The Disabled Persons (Services Consultation and Representation) Act acknowledged that disabled people need to have access to independent advocates. Although the relevant sections of the Act have never been implemented, the legislation has reinforced the importance of the role played by independent advocacy groups in lobbying and campaigning for single and collective causes. The requirement that local authorities must be seen to be consulting with end-users of services has also been reinforced by recommendations in *Health of the Nation* (HMSO 1992) initiative which has stressed the importance of gathering the views of service users and opportunities for access to independent advocacy.

Challenges and issues for advocacy services to address

One of the main functions of an advocacy service has become the requirement to help people interpret the changes that have taken place in the provision of services. There is a need to translate the official 'jargon' which has developed as health and social services have moved towards commissioning services in the market place formed by the split between purchasers and providers. Language is often a major barrier to people accessing the services they need. Social care services now apply the language of the finance markets to describe both their infrastructure, personnel and the implications for users who are now custom-ers. This uncomfortable association of personal care with the language of accountancy means that people become statistics, and cuts in services become cost-saving 'measures' and 'down-sizing'. It is alien to most people.

Research (e.g. Berrington *et al.* 1996; Chapman *et al.* 1997) also indicates that there is an extensive need to develop both access to, and interpretation of, information about the range of services available to disabled people in community settings. The 1990 Community Care Act was supposed to ensure that responsibility for coordinating support and access to services for indi-viduals with disabilities was to be placed in the remit of one agency. Social Services Departments were given this statutory responsibility. Understand-ably, departments have neither the time, nor the levels of knowledge, to meet this challenge completely. There is finally the fear and suspicion that accom-panies the concerns of individuals when personal circumstances become part of professional discourses.

Social workers have traditionally seen themselves as advocates for a range of service users, including people with disabilities; it is often why people have joined the caring professions. This can lead to a somewhat proprietorial sense of territory for both the social worker and the individual concerned, which in turn can lead to resentment of 'outside' people meddling in what they feel they both know best. The changes in the conditions of service for those in-volved in the caring services has nevertheless made it more important, rather than less, that independent advocacy is available to vulnerable people. How-ever, it is important to remember that most professionals and administrators have never been truly independent and so can never be true advocates. As the agenda for social work and care moves increasingly towards the rationing of services, the atmosphere and environment of professional concern has changed. Social workers are increasingly perceived as the withdrawers rather than the providers of services, and the internal market places an emphasis upon assessment of disabled people as clients, rather than helping them to provide a better quality of life for themselves.

Summary

In this chapter it is argued that quality of life is best judged by the way in which we treat people at the margins. Quality of life measures are made up from a complex array of variables that have become increasingly challenged by the imposition of the internal market. Quality of life is nevertheless central to the provision of services for disabled people, and the enhancement of subjective and objective measures of well-being remains an overarching goal of all who work in the caring services. For people in developing and impoverished economies, the promotion of community-based rehabilitation is considered to be one way of developing self-help for, and a communal commitment to, disabled people.

Finally, the tension between community-based rehabilitation and self-advocacy is examined, together with some of the reservations about what it is really possible to do for other people.

CHAPTER 5

Euthanasia and the new eugenics

Questions

- Is it reasonable for society to support the findings of genetic scientists in relation to the lives of disabled people?
- How is it possible to develop a positive recognition of disability whilst accepting a mother's right to choose to abort a foetus?
- Is it legitimate to practise population control?
- What are the implications of 'the right to die' in relation to the lives of people considered to be in a permanent vegetative state?

Introduction

Eugenics: the study of production of fine human offspring by control of mating. (*Concise Oxford Dictionary*, 1989, p. 104)

I have known so many women whose lives were devastated by having to take care of a helpless elderly parent or spouse. And of course, I have read about, or heard about many more . . . Proponents of the welfare state may object that in a properly run country, it should never be necessary for anyone to become a burden upon anyone else. That if one does become decrepit, one ought to be properly cared for by trained professionals at the public expense. But, I ask you, is such a utopian solution realistic? ('Do we have a duty to die?', *Voluntary Euthanasia Society Newsletter*, January 1988)

The sex instinct in defectives is often violent and unrestricted; and in a feeble-minded male, may lead to outrages as brutal as they are repulsive. Healy (an American eugenicist) goes so far as to urge a drastic surgical operation, not merely to prevent the creature from propagating others of his type, but also to root out these vicious inclinations from the criminal himself. (*The Young Delinquent*, Burt 1925, p. 319)

The natural in man is due to inborn heredity, the cultural to his acquired heritage. Congenital heritage is received during gestation, perinatal and post-natal at the moment of birth and throughout human education. (*Wolf Children and The Wild Boy of Aveyron*, Malson and Itard 1972)

The late nineteenth century saw the emergence of the consideration of eugenics as a science, but the construct has a longer history. As we approach the end of the twentieth century, the issue of eugenics has moved from the narrowly defined definition of heredity towards issues related to pregnancy, abortion, euthanasia and genetic engineering. The aim of this chapter is to expand the debate away from the perception of genetics as a dangerous science and to focus instead on gene technology as a dimension of effective therapeutic strategies and personal choice.

Whilst human behaviour may not depend on heredity alone, the system of biological needs and functions carried by the genotype are passed on at conception and relate us in some way to all other living creatures. How much of an individual's intellectual ability is determined by environmental factors and how much is already decided by a person's genetic make-up is one of the oldest debates in the area of Disability Studies. Heredity may set the limit that one may reach in intellectual capacity, but the environment determines how close one comes to achieving the potential within us all. The relationship of genetics to the circumstances of people with disabilities brings us to a consideration of the capricious workings of the laws of mutation and the principles of inheritance, dominance and recessive genes.

There is a long history of attempts to build the case for a congenital link between criminal and/or moral deviancy, and educational backwardness and mental retardation. This was particularly prevalent at the beginning of the twentieth century. Goddard (1912) made a careful, but ultimately selective, study of two lines of descent traced from Martin Kallikak – one 'normal', the other 'feeble-minded'. Kallikak is reported to have been a soldier in the American Revolutionary wars by some writers (Ray 1983), but is more likely to be a pseudonym contrived by Goddard from the two Greek words *kallos* for beauty and *kakos* meaning bad, to cover investigations into an extended family line. Martin Kallikak fathered both a legitimate line of children and an illegitimate son with an innkeeper's daughter, or tavern wench, and so started two parallel lines of descent. The members of his legitimate family were judged to be psychologically normal, whilst the offspring of the illegitimate line were deemed to be full of mental defectives. A similarly notorious study is the investigation of the Jukes family (Dugdale 1877). The descendants of Max Jukes, who was described as a drunken vagabond from the backwoods of New York State, were traced by Dugdale. By 1915 they totalled 2,094 people and amongst them were claimed to be 140 convicted criminals (seven of whom were murderers), 300 prostitutes, 310 beggars and 600 cretins. In more recent times this theme, linking criminality with reduced levels of intellectual ability, has been resurrected. For example, the racist claims that blacks are intellectually inferior to whites as a result of inherited characteristics has been raised by Herrnstein and Murray (1994) in their provocative account of the dispersion of IQ. At the time of writing, the Nordic policy of forced sterilisation on people with developmental disabilities as practised in Scandinavia between 1934 and 1976 has been exposed (Guardian, 3 September 1997, p. 13). It is a reminder that delusions of racial purity lurk just beneath the surface of the collective human psyche.

The study of genetics is complicated by more than spurious and racist judgements; there are a number of more central ethical and practical dilemmas related to the families of people with disabilities. Geneticists are first of all unable to experiment directly on human subjects and so tend to work with the short-lived, but prolific and more readily available, fruit fly. The study of genetic make-up is also complicated by the sheer complexity of the genetic structure of the human species. The number of genes involved and under investigation must be numbered in tens of thousands and this is before account is taken of possible combinations that may arise. Breaking it all down into distinguishable traits that can be mapped and analysed is the purpose of the human genome project.

The human genome project

The human genome project was started in the United States in the 1980s to trace and map out the genetic structure and variability of the entire human population. In effect, this worldwide exercise in mapping the structures that make up human biology is liable to change medicine from pure disease management to prevention of individual risks. It thus has the potential both to forecast and to eradicate impairment and disability through biological therapy and improved understanding of the construction of genetic material. At this point it is probably worth recalling that the nucleus of a normal human cell contains 23 pairs of chromosomes, making a total of 46 chromosomes altogether, and as is well known, a human being is formed from these 23 pairs of chromosomes. Chromosomes are composed of the essential genetic material, genes. Each gene within 22 of the chromosome pairs has a duplicate gene in the 'matching' chromosomes; the twenty-third pair is sex-linked, and its genes may be identical (XX for females) or different (XY for males). Research to date indicates that these chromosomes provide each of us with some 80,000 genes. The average gene has 2,000 base pairs; of the expected 80,000 genes only 6,000 are known, i.e. less than 10 per cent (Hameister 1996).

The sheer enormity of the project can perhaps be better understood when it is realised that only 5 per cent of the human genome is currently under investigation. 'The other 95% of the genome is still unknown' (Hameister 1996, p. 32). At the dawn of the genome project, molecular geneticists often focussed on simple genetic diseases. For example, in one of the first important accomplishments of positional cloning (the process that is now widely used to link genes to traits) researchers in 1983 found a location on chromosome 4 linked to Huntingdon's disease. 'This kind of one gene, one disease formula, enticed scientists with the prospect of making relatively easy progress in the understanding and treatment of inherited diseases' (Allen 1997, p. 34).

Such optimism has turned out to be something of a false dawn. Other key linkages have been proclaimed and either dismissed or quietly forgotten: an obvious case is the controversial 'discovery' in 1993 of a homosexuality gene. It may be that some diseases are relatively easy to account for, Huntingdon's disease and sickle cell anaemia among them, but the variations in the gene mutations may be so large and involve so many other variations and combinations as to be almost unknowable. However, whilst the spectre of a relatively simple genetic determinism may be disappearing within the scientific community, this does not mean that the spectre of a genetic basis for a whole raft of disabling conditions can be dismissed from the collective psyche of the general population. This populist argument for genetic determinism has guided many people's atavistic judgements in relation to disablement, phobias, neuroticism and the wish to exercise control.

Moral and ethical considerations

It would normally be accepted that ethical principles should be closely related to legal consequences. Ethics, or 'the principles by reference to which we organise our lives and decide what we ought or ought not to do' (Kennedy 1980), are not therefore the preserve of any one group. However, as a result of their day-on-day involvement with disabled people, doctors, care workers, social workers and managers tend to be delegated to make judgements about other people's lives. This is expected of them; they are held responsible for knowing what ought to be done. It would, therefore, be comforting to believe that the judgements made are based on the technical expertise and training that they have received. It is, nevertheless, unlikely that all the decisions made about the lives of disabled people are technical, or that they are a matter for any one profession alone. The judgements to be made are fine judgements of truth and honesty and whether or not these principles can be waived. Moral and ethical determination lies at the heart of the approval of society and these judgements rely more upon the prevailing cultural and spiritual values of society than any technical expertise.

Is it a doctor's responsibility alone, for example, to decide whether it is ethically correct to treat a baby born with a severe impairment when, if untreated, the baby will normally die through what has come to be called benign neglect? Such dilemmas of moral judgement also arise each time a social worker has to decide on the needs for respite care, or a doctor weighs up what to do with an elderly person paralysed by a stroke; it applies to the disabled person, with deteriorating eyesight, living alone in their own home. As Kennedy stated in his Reith Lecture, 'There is no mechanic's manual, no technician's guide, which indicates when treatment is justified' (Kennedy 1980). What happens instead is that professional judgements are made on the basis of some rough and ready index that anticipates an individual's future 'quality of life'. These life and death decisions are not technically determined but more often fashioned around human fallibility.

For people with disabilities the human application of genetics carries with it a variety of ethical and practical risks. Scientists are clearly interested in the overriding concern to see the use of bio-technology in the diagnosis and cure of genetic disease. But there are commercial and industrial outcomes to genetic medicine that cannot be ignored. For families at risk of genetic conditions that may contribute to impairments, the implications of genetic engineering are somewhat confusing and disturbing. For example, some British GPs are refusing to take disabled people on to their lists because they are seen as financial drains on the budgets of fundholders (Rock 1996, p. 121), and it has been suggested that life insurance companies may begin to demand that people undergo genetic testing as a condition of insurance. Thus, insurers may begin to take a harder look at the premium loadings of people who have already had genetic tests (*Guardian* 20 February 1997, p. 14). Both the Association of British Insurers and the National Consumer Council are concerned that there should be no practice of identifying policyholders of life insurance who are at risk of genetic disorders (Gillott 1997).

The fear that this might serve to create a 'ghetto' of such policyholders of life insurance is unlikely. Life insurance tends to be taken out by people in their adulthood when a progressive disabling condition is most likely to be already evident. The premium loading will have been set accordingly. The real insurance risk lies with long-term illness and permanent health insurance as it falls increasingly upon the individual and less upon the state. This has been particularly noticeable in the United States (Allen 1997, pp. 29–36).

Clearly arguments about and related to the ethics of genetic research, fertility treatment, reproductive technology and abortion are not new. Added to this are the implications around genetic cloning, following the break-through treatment in the creation of Dolly the lamb born from a test tube conjunction of an embryo and the cell of an adult sheep (*Guardian* 1997a: 7; *Guardian* 1997b: 6). There is no practical reason why it should not now be technically possible to clone, or grow, a new human being from the fusion of a cell from a human adult with an egg. However, the creation of a new genetic underclass of human beings is unlikely, as well as being morally unacceptable. The method is likely to be used more helpfully to treat a range of life-threatening conditions. For example, if someone has bone marrow problems, a cell could be extracted from the body and fused with an egg which would then be fertilised. Fresh bone marrow cells could be extracted from the resulting fusion and put back into the body where healthy bone marrow could grow.

The relationship of eugenics theory to disability

Historically, eugenics has certainly existed as a deliberate response to control unwanted impairments since the Greeks and their mythology. Artistic portrayals of procreation between the gods and earthly mortals in a union of bodily perfection, practical accomplishment and intellectual agility are exhibited in art galleries and literature. The Greek civilisations, obsessed with bodily perfection, also served to justify the practice of abandonment and death, through the exposure of newborn babies considered to be imperfect. This ultimate form of subordination of disabled people continues today in a variety of more diluted forms of prejudice.

Barker (1983) has provided a well-argued analysis of the belief systems that underlie eugenics theory. In summary, he indicates the three assumptions upon which the proposition is built:

- human characteristics could be determined by inheritance according to laws that are knowable;
- it was possible to identify 'desirable' and 'undesirable' human characteristics;
- social policy should encourage the increased fertility of those with 'desirable' characteristics.

Desirability, as bodily wholeness, has historically remained in an image of masculinity and male dominance. The physically strong, lean and active male body is contrasted with the traditional and stereotypically passive female body. The female is doll-like, acted upon, dressed and undressed. Feminists suggest that this desire to manipulate the body is reflected in the institutional motives of the fashion, health, and pornography industries (Marris 1996; Wilson 1985, p. 3).

Biological determinism continues today in the life histories of thousands of disabled people who have lived through the brutal realities of institutional conformity and prejudice. The renewed threat to the 'right to life' of disabled people has also re-emerged as the implications of the human genome project come to be more widely considered and understood. Some commentators see this project as a breakthrough in gene therapy whilst others in the community of disabled people fear that it 'has given massive impetus and renewed rhetorical weight to the claims of biological determinism' (Shakespeare 1995, p. 23).

The practical reality beyond any discourse about the right to life (and the right to die) is the very deliberate killing of people at either the beginning or the end of their lives. Disabled people and their parents are at the centre of this. Proponents of this killing claim it to be justified on the grounds that disabled people are surplus to the requirements of society. The debate has become more urgent as scientific knowledge begins to move more rapidly in advance of both our moral interpretations of the findings and the legislative processes that frame their resolution. Furthermore, the term 'new' eugenics highlights some of the ethical dilemmas that face us all in relation to the sort of global society that we are becoming.

The oppression of disabled people occurs across different cultural groups and manifests itself in different ways. Racism is the most obvious example of stereotyping and discrimination based on and shaped by prejudice. The pseudo-scientific ideology of racism that has been used as a justification for institutional oppression of black people has its parallels in the power and prejudice of eugenics as a justification for the covert exploitation experienced by people with disabilities. The attempts to construct a science of measurement formed around the genetic basis for intelligence and human potential has shaped much of the history of disabled people in the twentieth century. The relationship between statistical science and eugenics links the statistician Sir Francis Galton with his cousin Charles Darwin – whose notion of the evolutionary advantage of the fittest forms the basis for eugenics. The possibilities for a scientific explanation of intelligence, rather than divine intervention, caused an explosion of interest in attempts to measure differences. Galton seriously believed that 'the heredity-chances of becoming famous are twenty-four times greater for a child with a famous father' (quoted in Malson and Itard 1972, p. 16). He also believed that it was possible to determine a gene for intelligence and that 'survival of the fittest' required the elimination of 'defective stock' in society.

The rejection of disabled people in its most extreme form has been dramatically advocated in the ideology of fascism. The fascist glorification of the 'perfect' human being resulted, under Hitler, in a deliberate effort to exterminate disabled people as 'imperfections which contaminate the genetic stream' (Coleridge 1993, p. 45). The Nazi euthanasia programme attempted to justify the elimination of disabled people on the grounds that they made no contribution to society and were a drain on resources; they were perceived as 'useless eaters' of resources without capital to contribute to the human lot. The Nazis and eugenicists may belong to history, but the emergence of newer forms of social Darwinism continue the assumptions that only the fit and fully functional have a right to real life (see Levine 1985).

The false logic of eugenicists who attempt to link the deterioration of social order in society with the size of families and unchecked reproductive practices has been ruthlessly exposed (e.g. Gould 1996). However, renewed interest in biological determinism is evident in the reactionary responses of the new right and 'back-to-basics' biology, encouraged by the mass media and spurious academic research studies such as that by Herrnstein and Murray (1994) linking IQ with class, race and genetic causation.

Opposition to genetic diagnosis

The traditional position of those opposed to abortion is centred around a concern for the status of the foetus. Abortion is thus part of the agenda of genetic testing and reproductive technologies. From the perspective of disability rights an additional argument emerges around the status of disabled people in society. The disability rights agenda opposes genetic diagnosis on the grounds that it devalues the lives of disabled people. There are clearly value judgements implicit in the decision that it is better to be born free from a known impairment than to have one. Genetic testing, like ante-natal screening, gives families the option of avoiding having a child with a known impairment or genetic condition.

The criticisms of genetic testing have also centred around the question of parental choice in relation to pre-natal diagnosis. It has been argued that choice is a consequence of the process of diagnosis and the technology employed rather than a moral decision. Parents themselves become de facto practising eugenicists: 'when medical interventions are particularly heroic, as with infertility treatments, foetal surgery and embryo genetic screening, women can find themselves having "chosen", yet feeling that it was not "this" that they wanted' (Rose 1994, p. 175).

Rose has argued that these choices are eugenic in their nature because they are premised on the marginalised status of disabled people: 'the underlying message is "screen, abort or fix." For this discourse, both the rights of disabled people and the complexity of decision are undervalued. The old and powerful mechanism of devaluing the victims and blaming mothers has been activated and can run and run' (Rose 1994, p. 196).

Beck (1995) equates the medical avoidance of genetic disorders with the more explicit eugenic removal of people with genetic diseases, as practised by the Nazis. His argument is that genetic testing is a form of contemporary barbarism to which society has not yet awoken: 'It gains access through the clinics, laboratories and factories of the new biochemical industries. Its victory parade does not begin with street brawls, the persecution of minorities or people's assemblies, the dissolution of parliaments and the abolition of constitutions. This time it steps on to the stage of world history dressed in white coats, of self-confident research, the good intentions of doctors and the desire of parents to do their "best" for their children' (Beck 1995, p. 32).

It is clear that concern for the rights of disabled people is a particularly powerful influence on the debates around abortion and genetic testing. Contemporary commentators continue to support a woman's right to choose in relation to abortion. However, as the Genetics Interest Group have pointed out, worries about the rights of disabled people have been woven into the argument alongside the related concerns that modern genetics is creating a society in which people are intolerant of anything less than perfection. The experience of the Genetics Interest Group is that parents who use genetic diagnosis to avoid the birth of a child with a genetic condition, after having a first child with the condition, love the child no less as a result of the choices they have made (Genetics Interest Group Briefing Paper, December 1996).

Euthanasia

Eugenics and euthanasia are not new. The premeditated extermination of disabled people has a long and shameful history. Both philosophies gather their strength of argument from associations with medicine and have as their premise an assumption that human social actions, of necessity, must be regulated. The theory of eugenics can be traced back to the belief that all human social action arises from genetic endowment and inherited characteristics. However, euthanasia is arguably the more insidious doctrine, seeking to justify the assisted murder of disabled and elderly people on economic grounds and medical expediency. Both are essentially socio-biological, medical and individualistic theories that continue the process of placing the ultimate responsibility for fitness to live on the state of health of an individual, rather than the environmental and social inequalities which cause them to be in pain.

The development of medical science in the area of genetics has given us the ability to both perpetuate and eliminate life. The act of deliberately killing a person can take place before birth, in the abortion of a human embryo, or in the withdrawal of life for a demented elderly person. The discourses around euthanasia perpetuate and extend the personal tragedy model of disability that has already been alluded to.

Although neither is currently legal in the United Kingdom, euthanasia and infanticide are widely advocated in discourses around the quality of life. In Australia's Northern Territory, the right 'to die with dignity' through voluntary euthanasia was legalised in July 1996 and has helped four individuals achieve a legally agreed form of assisted suicide. This legally sanctioned right for terminally ill Australians to commit suicide with a pill or lethal injection has subsequently been overturned, less than a year later in March 1997, after being contested by the Church, Aborigines and doctors (*Guardian*, 20 March 1997, p. 15 and *Guardian*, 25 March 1997, p. 3). Other concerns about patient consent in relation to legally sanctioned forms of doctor-assisted suicide have arisen in Oregon on the northern Pacific coast of the USA and in the Netherlands where mercy killings within strict legal guidelines can be carried out, although euthanasia is technically illegal.

The moral and practical complexities of mercy killing are best exemplified in relation to people considered to be in a permanent vegetative state (PVS). The case of Tony Bland, who died in 1993, having survived the football ground tragedy at Hillsborough, Sheffield, in 1989, has paved the way for a series of 'right to die' cases. Bland had his life-support terminated following a judgement in the High Court that he had no useful cortical function. However, euthanasia is too controversial an issue to be decided on the basis of case law. Other cases, since Bland, have shown that some recovery of function is possible even in the most severe cases. Jean-Dominique Bauby, the editor of *Elle* magazine, who died following a stroke, managed to dictate/type a manuscript of 130 pages (Bauby 1997) using the only part of his body that he could use, his left eyelid. Andrew Devine, who was massively injured in the same football tragedy as Tony Bland, has, eight years after the incident, started to become aware of his surroundings and is communicating with his family through a series of presses on a touch-sensitive switch (*Guardian*, 26 March 1997, p. 1). At the same time and almost in the same week as the Devine revelation, another family was seeking a legal declaration to discontinue the life-sustaining support for their daughter who had been diagnosed as suffering PVS (*Guardian*, 21 March 1997,

p. 12). Such tragedies as these show how diagnosis is, in itself, part of a continuum of severity. Andrew Devine was never considered to be as seriously-brain damaged as Tony Bland; however, while misdiagnosis of any condition is serious, misdiagnosis in the case of PVS is particularly alarming and too awful to contemplate. The challenge facing clinicians is to ensure that any acceleration of death for terminally ill people in extreme pain is properly debated on both clinical and moral grounds.

In the case of people with impairments, assumptions about the 'inevitable' poor quality of life have influenced the development of pre-natal screening and abortion. The express aim of screening, such as amniocentesis, is to offer abortion where impairment is indicated (section 1(i)(b) of the 1967 Abortion Act permits abortion if 'there is substantial risk' of the child being born with a severe handicap). At the same time there are clear financial 'costs' associated with the 'right to life'. As long ago as 1985, during a House of Commons debate on abortion, Peter Thurnham MP stated 'that to abort a handicapped foetus could well save the country one million pounds over the course of a life time'. However, while it is true that disability can amount to high economic costs, the level of debate might be better served if more consideration were placed on improved effectiveness in the distribution of resources rather than on absolute costs. As has been pointed out, where foetal screening indicates impairment, 86 per cent of the general public in Britain 'approve' of abortion (de Crespigny with Dredge 1991). 'Screening is rarely offered so that parents can plan for their child. These approaches have created a huge research industry and foetal screening and abortion are now major users of impairment- related resources' (Crow 1996, p. 64).

Summary

The foetal screening for abortion and the implicit acceptance of infanticide for babies with significant impairments are based on assumptions that the lives of disabled people are not worth living. Discussion of medically assisted suicide and living wills has exposed the same assumptions about euthanasia and the resources required to keep disabled people alive. This demonstrates the tension and paradox in the 'quality of life' debates in relation to disabled people. The re-emergence of the medicalisation of disability in the form of genetic testing suggests that the multiple experiences of disability are forms of difference-within-difference and this needs to be better understood. The social restrictions of external barriers are central to the social model/definition of disability. However, as has been noted in Chapter 1, impairment *is* relevant. For some individuals impairment as well as disability causes disadvantage.

Any attempts to reject or diminish the impact of medical interventions within a multi-faceted social construction of disability can only serve to illuminate some of the misunderstandings about Disability Studies. This tension is echoed in conservative academic circles that fail to see a clear rationale for Disability Studies as a discrete discipline. It is either part of psychology, or part of sociology, or at best perceived to be a cross-disciplinary exploration into the margins that exist in society.

If the multiple experiences of illness, impairment and social restriction are not acknowledged within Disability Studies, including the moral dilemmas that surround the right to life, the disabled people's movement lays itself open to misinterpretation and misappropriation. The concerns of disabled people about genetic screening and euthanasia have been used to strengthen the arguments of pro-life groups, and this does not necessarily promote a wider understanding of the purposes of the disability movement. As Crow reminds us:

> Although mainstream interventions are presented as being for the benefit of disabled people, in fact they are made for a non-disabled society. Ingrained assumptions and official directives make it clear that there is an implicit and sometimes explicit, intention of population control. Abortion, euthanasia and cure are presented as 'quality of life' issues, but are also justified in terms of economic savings or 'improvement' to populations (Crow 1996, pp. 64–5).

CHAPTER 6

The emerging politics of disability

Questions

- What distinguishes a politics of disability from other forms of politics?
- Why do we need a politics of disability?
- What are the principal components of a politics of disability?

Introduction

This chapter seeks to outline the development of the politics of disability: from charity to the 'deserving', dependent and disadvantaged, to the empowerment of a 'minority' who are discriminated and prejudiced against in an able-bodied society. In order to simplify a complex recent history of legislative reform, political struggle and developing radical ideas, it presents the changing politics of disability in five models, in a broadly chronological order:

- liberalism, conservatism and the 'deserving' dependent disabled
- post-war social democracy, welfarism and state-directed citizenship
- the disability movement, the struggle for rights and equal opportunities
- the resurgence of liberalism, New Right citizenship and the duty to disabled people
- the radical retort: Marxism and radical democracy as paths to empowerment.

These five models give an understanding of the range of options for the politics of disability. These options can be differentiated by three critical themes, which will be outlined prior to exploring the models:

This chapter was developed in collaboration with Paul Reynolds, who should be acknowledged as the principal author.

- the shift in focus from individual pathology to social change
- the shift in focus from legislation and individual rights to collective citizen rights and empowerment
- the shift from *doing for* the disabled to disabled people *participating in* political decision making.

These themes are important in identifying key shifts and developments in the development of a politics of disability which enables us to begin to answer the questions above.

The politics of disability: critical themes

The emergence of a distinctive politics of disability came from the larger social transformations and political struggles of the 1960s. Driedger (1989) claimed that the disabled movement was 'the last in a long series of movements for rights – labor, black, colonised people, poor people, women – and now people with disabilities' (p. 1). The development of a disability movement politics created a divergence between the policy community – charities, interest groups, clinically defined and categorised self-help or voluntary support agencies and policy bureaucrats within state agencies – and disabled activists in three respects.

First, there has been a shift in the contemporary conception of disability from personal tragedy and impairment to a broader social critique of able-bodied society. Focusing on the individual or their disability in the personal tragedy model confined the politics of disability to deciding on and administering policy provision and services to a passive, dependent and different part of 'normal' society. The dissatisfaction of disabled people with policies and services was explained as poor policy-making or 'sour grapes' from those who did not get what they wanted and would not accept that in democracies not all wants can be met.

The shift to a critical analysis of the assumptions and prejudices of able-bodied society and preconceptions of normality and abnormality – or ability and disability – refused political debate. The agenda moved from service provision to social change through the recognition of disability rights and the need for disabled people to be *integrated and active*, rather than *marginalised and ministered for*, in their society. The powerlessness of disabled people and the social and economic inequalities they suffer began to be seen as directly related not to assessments of individual capacities, but to the ideas and values of able-bodied society, which perpetuated a political system which subjected disabled people to prejudice, discrimination and unequal life experience as part of its 'normal' functions.

Second, and related to this, there was a growing pessimism as to the scope for change through legislation and policy change, and a greater interest in initiating social change through political struggle which empowers people with disabilities. Focusing on the development of legislation, policy-making and service provision for any group involves generic discussions – there are similar approaches to policy development whether the subject is about disability, age, health, transport or any other areas. Disability is one of a number of categories of 'client' or 'customer' which can be inserted into the 'equation' for arguments about special preferences or necessity for public services. As Erlanger and Roth (1985) observe:

> disability policy is in fact an aggregate of a variety of policies, each with quite different origins and purposes . . . it has been most often seen as a subset of some other, more general policy area such as labor, veterans or welfare policy. (p. 320)

The development of legislation, policy and service provision for disabled people is therefore determined by civil servants and experts who approach these developments as they would any other policy problem – within the dominant cultural values and ideas of contemporary, able-bodied society. Disabled people are always preconceived as the 'minority', the 'different' or even the 'deviant'.

Oliver (1990, p. 3) noted that the development of disability politics has been in part about the transition from campaigning for services to campaigning for rights and liberties – from demands for individual service responses to the needs of different forms of disability to societal changes in meanings, values and attitudes for the benefit of all disabled people. This shift argued for a widening of the input of disabled people from disabled services and policies to the range of legislation, policy or political decision-making. The 'ends' of disability policy and services, whilst important in improving the quality of life of disabled people, were seen as important as part of the means by which rights and empowerment can be asserted. Oliver and Zarb (1989) regard the disability movement as developing significant influence in policy-making in Britain, to the point where they 'will come to have a central role in counter-hegemonic politics and the social transformation upon which [disability politics] will eventually be based' (p. 237). Disability politics, then, is about political change and not simply policy 'wish-lists' – although the struggle for these 'wish-lists' is often the entry point for disabled people to become political.

Finally, but inextricably bound to the above, was the shift from the politics of disability; or from the administration *for* disabled people by experts, professionals, politicians and policy managers, to participation *by* disabled people in their struggle for empowerment or a more dignified advocacy. Participation in the struggles for disability rights – from attending and voicing concerns at local meetings of charities, self-help groups or local authority services to creating traffic blockages and being chained to the railings at the Palace of Westminster – is seen as a positive experience. Participation brings a rejection of marginalisation, personal dignity, collective support and solidarity and a greater visibility through which pressure can be exerted through media campaigns, lobbying politicians and mobilising public support.

These three factors are central to understanding the emergence of disability politics and of disability movements as political actors. Whilst that has created some divergence with the 'policy community', it does not exclude entering into processes and relationships that formulate legislation and policy provisions for disabled people. Driedger (1989) outlines the progress of disabled rights movements in developing an international movement (Disabled People International) which has embedded itself into the policy deliberations of international bodies such as the United Nations and UNESCO, as well as providing a structure for influencing national governments in concert with national rights organisations.

The distinction between disability interest groups and movement groups, nevertheless, is critical in understanding the politics of disability. It is centred around how disabled people 'plug into' the economic and political systems and social and cultural values and ideas which constitute society. Accepting a degree of overlap, it is evident in the propensity for interest group politics to work within a system which acts *for* disabled people (i.e. charities) and movement politics to be founded on the actions and ideas *of* disabled people. Oliver (1990) provides a useful typology which illustrates these structural differences in organisations: patronage *(for)*/partnership *(of)*, economic *(for)*/parliamentarian *(of)*, consumerist *(for)*/self help *(of)*, populist *(for)*/activist *(of)*, umbrella *(for)*/coordinating *(of)* (p. 117–18). He identifies four characteristics which are particularly distinctive of disability organisations as movements: a peripheral position in the political system; a critical view of the structure and ideological ethos of (able-bodied) society; post-materialist values; and an international agenda (p. 118–23). Oliver cites Liggett (1988) in assessing the relative costs and benefits of interest politics: 'in order to participate in their own management disabled people have to participate as disabled . . . the price of being heard is understanding that it is the disabled who are speaking' (p. 106).

Movement politics reject the entry of disabled people and their advocates into the policy forum in this powerless position. They argue for radical and participative struggle and the development of strategic alliances which focus on the vagaries of social inequalities. Alliance building is a positive politics in two respects. As Borsay (1986) cited in Oliver (1990) observes, struggle unites disabled people of all forms and extents of disability around a politicised agenda of disability rather than dividing them into their different categories of disability (pp. 105–6). Oliver adds that it offers linkage with other politicised 'minorities' such as ethnic groups, gays and lesbians and feminists, which opens up its radical potential for social change (pp. 127–33).

Participative politics also creates a bridge between the political agendas of activists and the development of legislation, policy and service provision and the personal worlds of disabled people themselves. It links with the subjective experience, values and attitudes of people with disabilities with political agendas for social change. Issues such as the suppression of the sexuality of many disabled people, or the subjective perception of charity services as reinforcing pathologies even as they provide welfare services, can be linked to policy and political decisions. This form of politics has been the focus for other critiques of oppressive or exclusive society – and 'mainstream' politics – such as feminist and anti-racist critiques, which stress that 'the personal is political'.

If these are the dominant characteristics of the politics of disability which has emerged since the 1960s, they have to be placed within their historical context. Many of these ideas rooted in the critical themes are part of a politics confined to academic radicalism and a minority of political activists. To understand the continuing persistence of the politics of the disability-policy community and its focus on services and policy provision, or presumptions of passivity and dependency which spread from public servants and politicians or charity workers or volunteers to disabled people themselves, there needs to be some understanding of how change in the larger political context of welfare, inclusiveness and rights in society has occurred. This context is sketched below in five stages, giving rise to five models.

Liberalism, conservatism and the 'deserving' dependent disabled

Prior to the development of the welfare state, disability was conceived as a product of individual personal tragedy. Whether this tragedy was by birth, accident or illness, it was regarded as something individually experienced and generally, from the industrial revolution onwards, wanting of sympathy and support – manifest by family care, charity or institutional incarceration in asylums or suchlike. Disability was regarded as *impairment* – it impeded the capacity of disabled individuals to live or act as able-bodied individuals, and so impeded their enjoyment of rights and liberties. Their disability rendered them 'invisible'.

This was reflected in the dominant ideologies of industrial society: liberalism and conservatism. Both of these ideologies provided interpretations of society propagated by those with power, whose interests they prioritised. Ideologies – as coherent sets of ideas and values which formed 'world views', or ways of looking at, interpreting and explaining the world – persuaded others to believe and be loyal to these dominant interests' 'world view' of the way society worked. Dominant ideologies defined and captured the status of 'common sense' or truth with their interpretation. As tools of persuasion, they sought to be inclusive across all segments of society unless they explicitly excluded – as with racist ideologies. Disabled people were in part 'invisible' to these ideologies because they had no power and their impairment deprived them of the ideal of the individual from which liberalism and conservatism built their picture of society. Those in power had an able-bodied perception of the world and gave only sympathy or contempt for the impaired.

Liberalism represents society as an aggregation of individuals, with society simply a product of the sum of all market transactions between these individuals. Individuals form private voluntary associations – family, business, social – and accept the need for a political authority – government – to maintain law and order. They are perceived as self-interested, free to enjoy their liberties and to choose to compete with varying success in the market – be it for property and wealth, partners or other forms of self-aggrandisement. In liberal society, individuals are idealised as educated, informed, enterprising and competitive in the market. Their rights are codified as 'natural rights' – life, liberty and property – with the assumption that their individual intent and effort, with the legal protection of a minimal state, will achieve just rewards.

Set against this liberal model, disabled people are impeded in their competition in an able-bodied society. The degree of their impairment corresponds to the degree of their impediment in acquiring knowledge, qualifications and the capabilities as individuals to take opportunities and make choices with positive outcomes. Disability therefore defines them outside of market society. The 'liberal individual' represents an ideal which disabled people cannot meet, so disabled people are regarded as 'lesser' individuals. Instead, the medical model of disability, supported by the morality of liberalism to offer individual charity or minimal state support, encouraged their definition as deserving and dependent.

Disabled people in a liberal society enjoy the status of individuals through the goodwill of those they depend on. The conditional nature of their 'join' with society formed a barrier between ability and disability which few could cross. Only if the disability was manageable and invisible, or they had money or the disability was caused by an act of social status – such as the maiming of an officer in wartime – could disabled people expect to be seen in the same way as individuals who were able-bodied.

Likewise, conservatism argues for conservation of the fundamental cultural and political character of society through adapting and absorbing change into a hierarchically ordered, socially authoritarian society, drawing identity from class, nation and race, through the monarchy, custom and tradition. Conservatism has been historically intertwined with liberalism in modern societies, preserving its individual liberties and market organisation of society within the context of the national community. Disabled people in modern societies became a part of an able-bodied hierarchy, largely powerless and the subject of paternalism through their 'deserving' status. Accident of birth might give different disabled people a life of sumptuous luxury or a life of institutional incarceration or poverty, but the autonomy of disabled people was strictly conditional on family or class position. Neither liberalism nor conservatism, regardless of the charity, compassion and goodwill expended upon disabled people, empowers them. They are locked into a structurally weak position in society, dependent, invisible and powerless.

Post-war social democracy, welfarism and state-directed citizenship

The development of social democracy after the Second World War changed this invisibility. It was founded on the development of the welfare state and an inclusive notion of citizenship in society, which involved a commitment to *social* justice, rather than *individual* care. Social Democrats – or Reformists – had a concept of society which recognises diverse minorities and develops a welfare and policy community to draw them into a supportive relationship with the state. The role of the state was central to the recognition of the needs and responsiveness to minorities. The ethos for change was 'piecemeal social engineering' – social change derived from the state responding to democratic demands from all social interests for a better society. The welfare state, funded by progressive taxation and so supposedly redistributing resources from rich to poor, exemplified the social justice implicit in social democracy.

T. H. Marshall (reproduced in Bottomore and Marshall 1992) defined the concept of citizenship for social democracy in his lectures 'Citizenship and Social Class'. The state was at the centre of this model, reflecting the democratic political will and safeguarding the civil/legal, political and social rights of the individual. It initiated the realisation of rights through legislation and policy, and was the enabler of rights by providing services. It acted as a focus for public duty and obligation to 'minorities', though personal charity was encouraged. It set the terms for inclusion through policy communities and service provision.

The extension of the welfare state, the development of professionalised state services for disabled people, and support for self-organisation by, and support organisations for, disabled people would seem to meet a disability politics agenda. This agenda, however, was largely written for, rather than by, disabled people. Whilst their voice can be heard, it is channelled into a care and support orientation which incorporated them rather than encouraging change within society to reflect their politics or identity. Levels of service become the measure of rights and liberties, and the focus is still individual – the benchmark of social improvement is still the enablement of individual disabled people or self-defining groups, through technology or advocacy which alleviates dependency. Oliver (1990, p. 78–94) identifies individualism and dependency as key constraints on the empowering potential of social policy.

The social democratic model was also limited in the tangential and consequential nature of rights. As Taylor (1989) observes, 'social relations must be situated in the context of underlying power . . . . These power relations structure the spaces of the market and the state and thus limit the extent to which either can fulfil the ideal of citizenship' (p. 23).

Social democratic citizenship implies that disabled people would have a voice in both acquiring and defining provision, but power remained with the experts and vested interests within or networked into the state, who determined the deployment of resources. Social democracy delivered social welfare, ensured political rights and preserved fundamental civil liberties, but did so retaining a focus on disabled people as individuals with impairment. Its limitations were in the lack of power which disabled people gained as citizens. The omnipresence of the state arguably *disabled* rather than enabled people with disability by treating them as objects of policy provision. A result can be policies which suit vested interests as much as disabled people – such as the scandal over profiteering from the *Motability* (disabled mobility) scheme in the late 1980s and early 1990s – or emerge from professional orthodoxies influenced by the medical model. Because this model of citizenship is based upon a reforming and not transforming society, it is vulnerable to the fundamental characteristics of society: in a capitalist society profit and wealth through participation in the market are primary objectives, and the economics of disability service provision is dependent upon the continuation of prosperity and acquisition for those who are powerful and wealthy. Disability rights are conditional to capitalist economics.

Within the context of 'able-bodied' capitalist societies, disabled people have neither market nor state power, but rather rely on the affordability of welfare and the altruism which capitalism can fund. Disability policies, therefore, become not just a feature of social welfare ideology, encouraging social cohesion, the idea of community and support for the democratic consensus, but also a form of social control and regulation which locks disabled people into a more benign but still unequal hierarchy. Oliver (1990) warned: 'to engage in an uncritical relationship to the state, is to risk at best, incorporation or absorption, and at worst, isolation and marginalisation, and perhaps, ultimately, oblivion' (p. 128). Oliver (1996) is equally clear about the development of welfare for disabled people in capitalist Britain:

> discrimination against disabled people is institutionalised throughout society and . . . welfare provision has compounded rather than alleviated that discrimination . . . providing welfare services on the basis of individual need has failed disabled people . . . providing welfare services on the basis of individual need has aided the process of excluding disabled people from society rather than facilitated their inclusion. (pp. 76–7)

The disability movement, the struggle for rights and equal opportunities

Social democracy and its model of citizenship was challenged in the 1960s by both the development of rights movements and political struggles which sought a more radical, egalitarian redistribution of power, wealth and resources, and the capacity for the welfare state to continue to meet social demands through an increasing tax burden. Egalitarianism and its extension of the idea of social justice brought the idea of equal opportunities to the fore of disability politics and policy in the late 1960s and early 1970s. Two models emerged, one which reflected the power of liberalism even in egalitarian thinking, and one the growth of a radical rejection of even social democratic ideas of social justice and greater social equality. These models – reforming and transforming – are nowhere better illustrated than in Jewson and Mason's (1986) dichotomous model of equal opportunities policies, represented in Table 6.1.

The elements of the two different approaches to equal opportunities they identified were:

1. *Principles* – ingrained notions of fairness and justice.
2. *Implementation* – social mechanisms or devices which translate principle into practice.
3. *Effectiveness* – consequences of implementation in bringing about outcomes congruent with principles.
4. *Perceptions* – extent to which these processes are believed to be fair and just, have been implemented and have proved effective.

Table 6.1   Elements of liberal and radical conceptions of equal opportunities policies (Jewson and Mason 1986, p. 312)

Elements of equal opportunities policies	Conceptions of equal opportunities	
	Liberal	Radical
Principles	Fair procedures	Fair distributions of rewards
Implementation	Bureaucratisation of decision making (e.g. training)	Politicisation of decision making
Effectiveness	Positive action	Positive discrimination
Perceptions	Justice seen to be done	Consciousness raising (e.g. training)

The subject of Jewson and Mason's work was racist prejudice, but their general concern was to point out the conflict and contradictions of these two models and underline how both models did not of necessity produce the outcomes intended – for example, radical policies did not guarantee radical outcomes.

The liberal model has dominated equal opportunities policy-making in Britain, with its central weakness in its strategy for equality being individual redress through legislation rather than institutional reform. Hence, recruitment and promotion procedures may change, but social ideologies do not. The focus remains on disabled individuals, and equality offered to individuals going through processes with no sense of the disabling nature of the wider social context of inequality, prejudice and impediment.

Radical equal opportunities does provide a framework for discussion of disabled people's experiences, needs and wants as a 'minority' suffering inequality. It focuses on what disabled people want – for example stressing the importance of advocacy and empowerment as a basis for a society with greater 'life chances' for disabled people. Its problem is that the politicisation and positive discrimination it advocates is against the interests of able-bodied society and alien to the liberal culture of society. Radicalism looks to social change through transforming social structures and institutions, which challenges the existing powerful interests and so draws their opposition. This is demonstrable in looking at employment recruitment. The liberal 'justice' of equal competition for employment is opposed by the radical argument that society has ingrained social prejudices that can only be countered by political intervention – so the bureaucratisation of an employment recruitment form might not alleviate prejudice. Political action, such as legislation that requires companies to employ more than marginal proportions of disabled people in all occupations in their workforce, is seen as more effective. This moves beyond the liberal positive action of taking prejudice out of the recruitment process by establishing social justice through advantage towards disabled people – positive discrimination. The aim becomes not simply to be seen as just in the individual recruitment process, but to change social consciousness by ensuring disabled people and their achievements are visible in society. For the individual able-bodied person, this advantaging of disabled people might disadvantage them – and liberals reject this – but radicals see the social outcomes as more just.

Equal opportunities has been important also in its redirecting of demands for rights. The 1975 Equal Opportunities Act has facilitated limited opportunities for disabled people, but more importantly has been a forerunner to disability rights legislative proposals in the late 1980s and 1990s.

Liberal equal opportunities focus on individual rights and redress and its failure to address the societal and structural penetration of pathologies of disability shows its weakness. The social scope of both models of equal opportunities, however, in understanding oppression and discrimination as a social and not an individual problem, has furthered disability politics, and the radical model underlined the need for the struggle for rights to involve social change and participative politics.

The resurgence of liberalism, New Right citizenship and the duty to disabled people

The second challenge to social democracy in the 1960s and '70s was the problem of balancing capitalist profit alongside social spending, which brought social democratic politics and Marshall's model of citizenship into crisis. The New Right, led by Thatcher in the UK and Reagan in the US, returned to liberal and conservative values and rejected welfarism, egalitarianism and state intervention in the 1980s. They contrasted the statist and reformist ethos of Marshall's citizenship with a market-oriented model of 'active citizenship'. This model focused on the rights and responsibilities of the individual and replaced the state with the market as access point and enabler of rights and responsibilities. As such, it returns to the liberal representation of disabled people – the 'deserving poor'. Need is measured against the inherent undesirability of welfare through the public purse, which narrows definitions of what 'need' is and allocates reduced resources to that need. The expectation is that family or charity will play a greater role in service provision. State disability service provision is seen as driven by professionals and client groups for their purposes rather than for disabled people – and increasingly contracted out to the market, at reduced public cost. More critically, the new right reject the 'dependency culture' of welfarism with repercussions for even the 'deserving poor' – such as increasingly stringent assessments of qualification for disability benefits rather than more time-limited employment and social benefits.

This model, which was prevalent up to the 1997 election and is still influential on policy, has the same weaknesses of liberal and conservative ideologies. Its terms of inclusion are the capacity to enter into and consume and contract in the market in able-bodied society – a site of prejudice, discrimination and disadvantage. Disabled people cannot meet the ideal of the active citizen – an able-bodied ideal – and so suffer reduced public funding and services and the persistent blockage of rights legislation which might reverse those reductions or enforce responsibilities upon the state. To social democrats and those who argued for equal opportunities it was a step backwards, but enabled them to reflect on the weaknesses of state-directed or equal opportunities-led politics. For others, the movement away from the limited politics of disability offered by social democracy and equal opportunities provided the radical critique that those in power in society benefited from, and preferred, the prejudicial views of disabled people.

The radical retort: Marxism and radical democracy as paths to empowerment

Radical theories – Marxism, feminism (as examples) and the like – offer a more constructive model for disabled politics because they seek to transform society and conceive liberty, rights and freedoms as socially constructed – rather than individually based – and socially denied by the exercise of power and oppression. They have not traditionally, however, aimed at the issue of disability – Marxists focus on capitalist production and class, feminists on male power and patriarchy. This is not to say that they do not have something to offer disabled people – the Marxist axiom 'to each according to their needs, from each according to their abilities' clearly does. They argue an intrinsic but poorly defined expectation that Marxist or feminist change will inevitably extend equality to disabled people, but do not address disability directly as an issue with its own pathologies and politics. Indeed, the presumptions of these perspectives are of able-bodiedness as the 'normal' condition in society. Radical theories offer social transformation, but within an able-bodied norm.

The work of Mike Oliver is particularly striking here. Oliver (1990, 1996) has used the Marxist idea of hegemony as a key concept in his understanding of the politics of disablement, citing Harbert (1988) in Oliver (1990): 'It is not necessary to be a Marxist to recognise that economic conditions have a significant impact on social behaviour and on relationships between different groups of individuals in society' (p. 25).

Hegemony is, in simple terms, the balance of the use of coercion and manufacture of consent through ideology by which the state defends the status quo of class rule in capitalist societies. Oliver (1990) sets the terms of the capitalist, able-bodied hegemony succinctly:

> The hegemony that defines disability in capitalist society is constituted by the organic ideology of individualism, the arbitrary ideologies of medicalisation underpinning medical intervention and personal tragedy theory underpinning much social policy. Incorporated also are ideologies related to concepts of normality, able bodiedness and able-mindedness. (p. 44)

Oliver (1996, pp. 126–44) argues for the need to develop a 'counter-hegemony' which retrieves a concept of disability from its present pejorative meaning, and builds a positive meaning for and by disabled people, which would form the basis of a politics of disability. This counter-hegemony would be a challenge to capitalist 'able-bodied' society, with the politics of disability becoming a strategic deployment of agitation and ideology in order to transform society from an oppressive site of disablement towards an egalitarian society which transcended the able-bodied/disabled divide (Oliver 1990, pp. 127–33).

For Oliver (1996), political struggle leads to empowerment, which is a collective process – individual empowerment is a process of negotiating individually experienced constraints, whereas collective empowerment is a political process of agitating for change in a prejudiced society. It does not imply that all disabled people undergo the same process of a shifting consciousness of their oppression and pathology in a society that ostensibly 'cares' in the provision of disabled services, but it does locate disabled people within a *social* process where the negotiation of their individual constraints leads to an awareness of socially constructed pathologies and constraints. Shakespeare (1993) shares this view in seeing the act of participating in political struggle as enabling in itself, as well as displacing statist bureaucracies in setting the agenda for provision and legislation for disabled people.

Marxism has been the principal form of radicalism to influence disability politics. It has also contributed to recent explorations into the concept of citizenship which have influenced left academics and activists in developing an alternate radicalism which might better suit disability politics – radical democracy.

Radical democracy emerged from disillusionment with the grand movements of labour and socialist politics that failed to develop a politics which enabled diverse communities within society – women, ethnic groups, those of a different sexual orientation, etc. It was also influenced by the challenge to statist and organised political systems and processes of modernity by participative and diverse movement politics. The central idea behind radical democracy is its inclusiveness of plural and diverse interests, brought together by a commitment to egalitarianism and social justice and a participation and adherence to democratic processes. This democracy involves empowering all communities, encouraging their participation in a decentred, more localised politics, and developing their civic spirit through a more direct relation to political decision making. The essence of citizenship becomes what citizens determine for it, provided it does not exclude or disempower the communities who participate in and adhere to democratic politics. This concept of citizenship, and of radical democracy itself, is formed and reformed by those who live it, through continuous democratic dialogue.

The model is quite attractive and does offer a focus on reshaping society, on rights and empowerment and on participation by all minorities. It might, therefore, be an attractive form of disability politics. It is, however, not without its weaknesses. It lacks theory of power and an analysis of how democratic dialogue will avoid inequalities developing from differentials in power between different groups. If people with disabilities are relatively powerless in contemporary society, by what means will they gain social and political power and in what sense will they be able to exercise that power against interests whose agendas clash with a disabilities agenda? The assumption that power will be dispersed across the democratic community is arguably optimistic. Further, there is the question of how far a society or community can embrace diversity. At what point will common ideas and ideologies which promote social solidarity surface and what will their impact be on minorities such as those with disability? Will baseline assumptions of ability still lead to pathologies of disability? Certainly, a constantly redefining democracy might be subject to public reactions such as the need to contain and constrain those with mental illness after some unfortunate episode of violence. Without a benchmark code of rights, such a model leaves itself open to rule by mass mobilisation. This model, whilst attractive, is still very much an abstract alternative.

Towards a politics of disability

Since the 1960s, the politics of disability has been characterised by a critical focus on able-bodied society, a participative politics which empowers disabled people and a focus on rights and social equality. It has been pursued through the development of citizenship concepts from social democracy to radical democracy, and reinforced by more legislative and policy-oriented debates around equal opportunities, against a backdrop of traditional ideologies which render disabled people dependent and invisible politically.

The development of a politics of disability into the twenty-first century is likely to continue to be associated with the idea of citizenship. Oliver (1996) noted the importance of the concept in his discussion of how disability groups have focused on citizenship and anti-discrimination law as central to their empowerment:

> disabled people have begun to redefine disability not as personal tragedy requiring therapy but as collective oppression requiring political action. Thus, for the former group, the history of citizenship can be seen as the achievement of certain political, social and civil rights for everyone. For the latter, disability is nothing less than the denial of basic human rights to certain groups in society. (p. 44)

Whilst citizenship as a concept deals with concerns of social inclusion, the relationship of disabled people with other segments of society and the relationship between disabled people and the political world, it has often applied to disability with a focus on welfare rights which is perhaps a weakness. Discussions of welfare rights and services inevitably direct themselves towards politics within the context of an able-bodied society rather than the terms of social transformation. Fagan and Lee (1997) take this point further when they note that citizenship models do give disabled people *formal* rights, but in the substantive experience of their everyday lives their impairment excludes them from an equal participation in society. Thus society *disables* them because it does not move beyond presumptions of able-bodiedness as a basic attribute of the individual in society. The concept of citizenship remains, however, a central element for a politics of disability, and a site for radical criticism of the present rights afforded disabled people.

Insofar as the politics of disability is transformative, it is also hegemonic. Oliver (1990, p. 2) identifies a key element of the politics of disablement as understanding the politics of social meanings, citing W. I. Thomas – 'if men define situations as real, they are real in their consequences' – in arguing the need for a shift in the meaning of disablement in society from an individual to a social context. The shift in focus from individual to social frames of reference is neatly summed up by Shakespeare (1993):

> Our real enemy is not individuals, but the system which divides us, which creates our disability, which makes it possible for others to profit from our exclusion: it's convenient and easy to highlight people, but the focus of our rage and our action should be the structures. (p. 32)

Increasingly, for academics and activists, it is a radical politics. The Blair government, with its concept of 'stakeholding' as a mechanism of social inclusion, offers little of specific value to disabled people. There may be marginally more resources and marginally wider services, and a culture of listening to what disabled people want. There may even be the passage of a Disability Rights Act. The struggle to change able-bodied society, however, will be barely begun by such an Act. Further, there are still those who feel that equal opportunities, or social democratic citizenship, or indeed the New Right, offer the most practicable models of policy provision, and reject the agenda of social transformation.

This brief and short survey concludes that the politics of disability is currently organised around the notion of a counter-hegemonic strategy against able-bodied prejudice. This will involve development of a radical concept of citizenship which breaks down the able/disabled dichotomy and the development of strategic alliances for radical change and the empowerment of disabled people by political struggle to challenge the pathology of disability as impairment. Equally, however, the politics of disability is still contested by proponents of the different models outlined, and this analysis is part of that debate, rather than standing above that debate. The radical critique has been attractive to academics and activists but many disabled people still work within established interest groups and have a more passive and limited idea of what they want in service provision, legislative change and representation. The 'emerging' politics of disability is still *emerging*, and has still to move from concepts and minority activism to the hearts and minds of disabled people more generally, as the twenty-first century approaches.

CHAPTER 7

Disability research

Questions

- What ethical questions does disability research raise for non-disabled people?
- Is the point of research to directly improve the circumstances of disabled people?
- How might it be possible to develop emancipatory research with all groups of disabled people?
- How do you interpret the term 'participant observation', in relation to disability research?
- If it is true that 'you have to be disabled to understand disability', what do you think this says about the values placed upon disability research?

Introduction

Research in relation to the lives of disabled people has developed in recent years and autobiographical accounts serve as a useful foundation for a fuller understanding of the study of disability. Research into disability has also been questioned for a variety of reasons. To some extent, this criticism has emerged as a result of the way in which the battle lines of research production have been drawn. People with disabilities and learning difficulties in particular have tended to be treated as objects to be studied and a problem for other people rather than as individuals with the ability to participate in a research exchange. There is also a tendency to see the purpose of research in the traditional terms of either being for or against the quantification of data. Quantitative data, in the form of scientific experiments or surveys, are associated with a relative 'hardness' of results; this contrasts with the so-called 'soft' data gathered from qualitative approaches more commonly associated with investigations that try to interpret people's lives.

Virtually all social science research is an attempt to reinterpret experience and to seek explanation through increased 'depth of understanding'. Thus, the distinction between quantitive and qualitative research styles is somewhat artificial. For example, if you were to try to explain what you are doing at this moment (i.e. reading this paragraph), you would find yourself drawn towards describing conscious decisions, meanings and intentions. These interpretations are extremely important, but they are not sufficient, by themselves, as an explanation of your actions. It is the interpretation of these various meanings that brings understanding and distinguishes the social sciences from the so-called natural sciences, such as mathematics or physics. The need to understand intentions, and how the past influences the present, lies at the heart of the distinct research methodology of the social sciences. The intention is to 'get inside' the situation being studied and attempt to interpret the intentions, purposes and habits of the participants.

If disability is perceived as an individual tragedy and medicalised, it lends itself to data collections that reinforce images of impairment and loss of function. This in itself can lead to a mechanistic quantification of results and it has shaped the interpretive value of survey data such as the OPCS census (e.g. Martin *et al.* 1988). On the other hand, any qualitative research which attempts to interpret and describe disability as a relative concept is also problematic. Until recently, there has been a tendency to shy away from discussions of the subjective experiences of disabled people. As has been suggested by Shakespeare *et al.* (1996), Disability Studies has tended to downplay the personal and focus instead on the structural, thereby tending to reproduce and shape the split between public and private discourses with which students of the social sciences are familiar. Indeed, one of the features that has emphasised the limited self-esteem of people with disabilities has been the reluctance to assume that disabled people have personal stories to tell of their private lives. As a consequence they have been denied access to the experiences that 'normal' society takes for granted. The work of Morris (1991, 1996), Scope (1994), Campbell and Oliver (1996) confirms that this is an erroneous assumption. As Shakespeare *et al.* (1996, p. 208) have observed, the narratives of disabled people can be a cathartic experience. The resolution of conflicts for disabled people may result in stories with different emphases. Things that are taken for granted by non-disabled people may create obstacles for disabled people. The environmental, political and emotional restrictions that create disability (and how these can be positively overcome) form the basis of most research in Disability Studies.

Disability research in the community

The paradigm for disability research that emerges from the social model (which acknowledges that social barriers are imposed by society) views the person with the disability as the decision-maker and at the centre of any research encounter. This paradigm has developed as a reaction to research into disability as sickness and tragedy. The primacy of the person with a disability is at the forefront, with emphasis on the shared identity of oppression with other marginalised groups. This poses questions for non-disabled researchers who form the majority of the research-active community. Wiseman (1978), by memorably describing the role of the qualitative researcher as a detective in a classic murder mystery, has inadvertently tended to reinforce this dilemma in relation to disability research:

> Starting with a few clues, the detective questions persons connected with the case, develops hunches, questions further on the basis of those hunches, begins to see a picture of 'what happened' start to emerge, looks for evidence pro and con, elaborating or modifying that picture – until finally the unknown is known. (Wiseman 1974, p. 317)

It can be argued that if such an approach is adopted it lays itself open to accusations of a number of abuses and miscarriages of justice. However, this would deny the place of sensitivity and interpretation in the creative reconstruction that is the research process. The qualitative researcher who is seeking narrative accounts is, necessarily, an investigator that moves into the private circumstances of people's lives and has the potential to, either deliberately or unintentionally, turn informants' lives upside down. In relation to research into the lives of disabled people, the approach emphasises the need to remain aware that an informant is neither simply a 'research subject' nor a metaphor for generalised oppression. For many disabled people, research into their lives has become an activity that is undertaken by those who have power and is imposed upon those who do not (e.g. Oliver 1996b). Research in such circumstances reinforces a sense of further oppression and the violation of personal experience. Booth (1996), however, has more recently argued that the narrative, or story telling, method of research is about to make a legitimate resurgence. The personal experiences and perspectives of people within oppressed groups have been excluded, for too long, from the traditional forms of academic discourse. Disabled people have until recently lacked the power to make their voices heard and conventional scholarship has tended to subordinate the reality of people's lives as anecdotal rather than serious scholarship.

In qualitative research the researcher is attempting to make valid sense of the social world, and of the people being studied. In their attempt to reinterpret what some people would describe as their everyday lives, researchers are also reconstructing and exposing often unacknowledged truths. As such, concerns arise for the validity and reliability of data. There should also be a sense of responsibility towards informants (which should be at the heart of any research). These considerations are of paramount importance in the development of analytic insights.

There are a number of pointers that the researcher in Disability Studies may use to help retain this sense of empathy:

- Assume, at least at first, that no one is lying in the information you receive.
- Acknowledge that there is no such thing as absolute truth. There are a variety of perspectives and room for a range of insights.
- Nothing that you see or hear is completely irrelevant to your study. It may serve to enrich a direction that you are already pursuing, or set you onto another topic.
- If you must choose between an official story and that of an individual (that is institution versus individual) it is likely that an individual is telling the more unblemished truth and that the institution is not being totally honest.
- Recognise that there is nothing that happens or that people tell you about that 'doesn't make any sense'. It is part of their lives and they think it makes sense.
- Assume that human beings may not be very sophisticated, or smart, in the decisions they make, but they are doing the very best they can under the circumstances.

The ethics of disability research

It is anticipated that all research is guided by sound theoretical principles and this is particularly the case in relation to investigation in connection with the circumstances of people with disabilities. Furthermore, both local and national government policy in relation to disability is anticipated to be informed and underpinned by sound research. Unfortunately, this is not always the case. French (1994a, p. 136) encapsulates the problems associated with disability research when she indicates that the way disability is defined sets the tone for any research project. The majority of large-scale research activity is quantitative in its nature and this reflects the level of funding allocated to such activity. This in turn tends to reinforce the notion that disability is something contained within the individual; that it can be estimated, quantified and extrapolated from survey data (e.g. OPCS surveys Martin *et al.* 1988). Such surveys imply that people with disabilities have to compare their levels of difficulty in, for example, reading a newspaper, or walking a hundred metres, with non-disabled people. Not only will this vary between the levels and types of impairment experienced, but it also suffers from the lack of a normal baseline against which to measure their efforts. 'Even basic facts such as the number of disabled people residing in a given place, are based upon the criteria used to define disability which, in turn, may reflect the interests of the researchers or their funders' (French 1994a, p. 138).

Social science research is presented as a neutral, value-free exercise, which is expected to result in the acquisition of factual data. The research that has emerged in relation to Disability Studies has tended to follow in this direction too. In reality, this independence and balance is a myth. The majority of research is carried out in university departments, or in association with universities and the influence of the body funding the research is often funda-mental to the direction of the outcomes; frequently these are directed towards policy that is itself ambivalent and demands further research. In relation to disability research in particular, the more radical proponents of a politics of disability would suggest that it is impossible, if not irresponsible, to remain neutral; you are either on the side of the oppressor, or on the side of disabled people. Research in this context should be assisting disabled people in their struggles (Barnes 1996). In such a climate it is important to realise that if a researcher tries to present an honest account of what is happening, it will often mean upsetting at least one of the parties involved: 'there must always be room for argument and counter argument and crucially for researchers, to reveal matters that may be uncomfortable, for specific interest groups and even those funding the research' (Bury 1996b, p. 112).

Representation

Representing the views of disabled people has often been difficult. Informa-tion and data on disabled people have formed the basis for numerous statistical reports. Indeed they have become the very stuff of acres of news-print related to the caring services and more occasionally they have been the subjects of best selling books and films. Sometimes too, disabled people have reached national attention through 'brave deeds' (such as pushing a wheel-chair from John o' Groats to Land's End) or as a result of some frequently painful, but always 'miraculous', intervention of a medical nature.

These stories and reports have been useful in generating our collective recognition of disabled people as victims of both internalised and externally generated oppressions; but they have not been told by disabled people themselves. Their lives have been interpreted, retold and packaged for the consumption of a society that still sees disability as a kind of personal tragedy, in which the able-bodied majority have custody of the lives of the people with disabilities. Until very recently, in effect, disabled people had very little opportunity to tell their own stories within the political and cultural contexts of their personal circumstances.

There cannot be any effective research into people's lives that is not to a greater or lesser extent autobiographical. Hevey (1992) and more recently Campbell and Oliver (1996) have reinforced this point, suggesting that it is ridiculous to believe that 'objectivity' can only exist outside personal consciousness. In other words, attempts to be objective have only served to hide the personal and distance the person from the text of their experiences. Oliver (1992, 1996b) has commented, more distressingly, that scientific, 'hard' social research has done little to change the status quo; neither improving the quality of life of disabled people nor having much effect on policy, legislation or social change.

> The problem is that most social research has tended to privilege methodology above experience and, as a consequence does not have a very good track record in faithfully documenting that experience; whether it be the black experience, the experience of women, the experience of disability and so on. (Oliver 1996b, p. 45)

Oliver (1992, 1996b), Campbell and Oliver (1996), and Bury (1996a, 1996b), have all argued that research in the area of Disability Studies should be seeking to break away from the shackles that restrict research paradigms to a simple dichotomy between survey and more qualitative methods. Research should instead attempt its own emancipation in both form and content. If disability research becomes confined by the definitions of disability as 'social oppression', with its inevitable distinctions between insider and outsider accounts, there is the danger of a number of unwanted consequences. There is the central concern of alienation and cynicism – both across the broad constituency of disabled people and within society in general. This, in turn, demands the formation of new alliances between researchers and their research subjects:

> the idea that research should become a site for 'struggle' suggests a politicisation of research that may have a number of unintended consequences. While it may be taken as axiomatic that individuals have a unique insight into their own experiences, it does not logically follow that they are qualified or able to undertake research. Moreover, such a view also runs the risk that the status of being disabled should be the main criteria for carrying out research on the subject. This sits uneasily in an argument in

which the very idea of 'disability', as a defining characteristic of individuals, is being challenged. (Bury 1996a, p. 35)

The research conducted by Campbell and Oliver (1996) is powerfully instructive in light of this discourse. As researchers and as disabled people they not only expose the inherent tensions between insider and outsider accounts, but also reveal the connections between disability research and research around other related movements, like the marginalisation experienced by gay rights campaigning groups.

Research that shows a connection between the dual oppressions that so often mask the real experience of disability has not often been undertaken. Shakespeare *et al.* (1996) have researched and explored some of the more hidden sexual experiences in the lives of disabled people and in this way innovative research also acts as a liberation which tells of shared oppressions and can reveal the extent of disabled people's anger and protestation. But such research is still in its infancy. Nevertheless, the ethnograhic, collective and private oral biographies that disability groups have begun to assemble provide an opportunity for disabled people to trace the history of their political consciousness, define their own issues and understand their own experiences (e.g. Berrington *et al.* 1996; Cartwright *et al.* 1996; Morris 1996). For such accounts to be included in the realms of research, they need to be publicly accessible and available. This often calls for funding for dissemination that is not always sufficiently considered when the original research proposal is first put forward. The vested interests of the researchers also need to be open to scrutiny and debate. For those who are interested in disability-related issues as an area of research but who remain as outsiders and allies, collaborative research would seem to be a way to withstand some of the suspicion that is associated with research and researchers in this area of the social sciences.

Conducting and writing up research in Disability Studies

Researchers in the social sciences have taken considerable interest in discovering which factors have the most influence in shaping the ways in which the members of different social groups interpret their situations. Ethnographic accounts, in particular, seek the opportunity to find out how different people conceptualise the social world in which they live. They also seek to respect the cultural and ethical values integral to the lives of their informants. Thus, students in the area of Disability Studies can usefully learn from the ethnographic traditions of research in the development of a life-history approach to disability awareness. This includes the perceptions of disabled informants, carers, service providers and so on. The development of a life-history anticipates that students will find out about people's images of themselves and of their social world. Since it requires that informants discuss and describe their perceptions in their own terms, it requires the researcher to interpret rather than to predetermine the agenda or structure of an interaction.

Tom Shakespeare (1996) gives an insight into the rules by which he conducts qualitative research. These generally coincide with aspirations that all researchers into disability issues might learn to put into operation. The aim is to give an accurate representation of the views of those involved in the research process, providing a sufficient and adequate explanation of the purpose of the research and providing the opportunity for participants to ask questions and to revise their statements. Any research interviews undertaken need not be rigidly structured; giving participants some say in the direction that is taken during a research exchange is important. In the writing-up phase and the development of a reflective account of disability research there is potentially some tension in that what has been uncovered should be presented in a form that is accessible to all; but it must also be able to withstand the rigours of academic criticism.

When carrying out any piece of research there can be pitfalls. In the social sciences, and Disability Studies in particular, the method chosen can affect the findings. The presence of the researcher can affect how people behave and the answers they give. For these reasons it is advisable to seek opportunities to carry out follow-up interviews with informants, in the hope that given the regularity of contact respondents will become more relaxed and feel more confident in expressing themselves freely.

The writing of biographies and autobiography is of course an ancient practice, but the life-history – the elicitation of semi-structured autobiographies for the purposes of social research – is of rather more recent origin. Life-histories were originally carried out by anthropologists studying the vanishing lifestyles of American Indian tribes (e.g. Benedict 1934) and were made famous by the Chicago School of Sociology. More recently the life-history approach to research has been encouraged in the form of oral-history with disabled people as a group and with individuals, e.g. Zarb (1993b) with older people; Shakespeare et al. (1996) on the sexual experiences of disabled people; Campbell and Oliver (1996) on the development of a politics of disability; Cartwright et al. (1996) with physically disabled people in the north west of England.

In ethnographic or life-history research, the interviewer rarely comes to the interview with a detailed agenda or questionnaire since the primary aim is to encourage informants to talk about their lives on their own terms. The fundamental point is to reduce the danger of the interviewer imposing their own opinions on their informants through the form of the questions posed. It is, nevertheless, impossible to take an entirely passive role when carrying out interview research. Informants are inevitably expecting to be guided by the interviewer, at least in the initial stages of any interview, and whenever there is a break in the talk it will be expected that it is the interviewer who 'will make the next move'. It is also the case that it is often in the best interests of the researcher to gently steer informants towards those areas of their lives which are considered most relevant to the research purposes. It is consequently useful to have decided beforehand on the general 'shape' of the information/ topical exchange and to have some questions prepared, both to get things started and to stimulate further relevant talk when things begin to flag.

Reflection

The imposition of ablist views on disability research is a concern that can both cause offence and prevent a proper understanding of disability being brought to a wider audience. While a shared understanding of disablement is often better informed and more sensitive as a consequence of research it is really only possible to touch people's lives briefly and not enter them. Only a disabled person can claim to have anything near to a similar experience to other disabled informants (e.g. knowing how important it is to plan a journey away from home around the availability of accessible public lavatories, which, as many research reports indicate, are often far from accessible and thus far from public).

The development of a research study involves all concerned in a range of experiences. From the outset, the intention should be to make use of the voice of the interviewee and to explore their perceptions of their daily lives. At the same time it has to be anticipated that, as consumers of services, the views expressed by disabled people may indicate varying levels of dissatisfaction. Non-disabled researchers may anticipate concern to be expressed by disabled people about being overlooked, made 'invisible' in a world that regards 'normal circumstances' as the ability to walk, remain ambulant, be articulate and aware. It can come as a shock to find this is not always the case. For some, the response to conflicts around provision and the meeting of need may simply result in acceptance, even gratitude, for the professional services that are offered and available.

A certain level of incomprehension about disablement can begin to establish itself at certain points for a researcher or research team. This tends to occur when researchers are unprepared for encounters, and conversations emerge that are not in accord with their own theoretical views. Some informants may perceive researchers as extensions of the very services that they either welcome or criticise, whilst others may assume that researchers are part of an advocacy service who are able to bring about instant change. There is sometimes the expectation of a quid pro quo or a quick research 'bargain' that can be negotiated by way of a swap – the individual 'story' of any one person's circumstances in return for advocacy, advancement, or immediate practical help. This can be both unexpected and unwelcome.

From the outset, disability research has to acknowledge the fundamental principle that the people who really know best about the experience of disability are disabled people themselves. It is evident, after a number of years as an ally, that this is not necessarily the same as being able to articulate a case for disabled people. What people know best is their own circumstances, and this does not have to include (or even acknowledge) impairment, handicap or disability. Thus, some people who appear to be living with a great deal of dependency on medical support may have little understanding of the cause of their functional impairment or its prognosis. Some who have been promised services may have been waiting for months or years to receive them. To a researcher, disabled informants in these circumstances should by now be getting angry, militant, and calling service providers to book. But the purpose of the researcher is not to appear to criticise, but to attempt to understand. If an informant appears to be disorganised, or in some cases lacking the will and initiative to take on 'authority', they may have consciously chosen not to! The function of the researcher into the life-histories of people is to record and interpret, not to prejudge.

The inclination to set about advocating for the individual rights and entitlements of informants is understandable, but out of keeping with the proper purpose of the research exercise. These are the frustrations that can be felt by the researcher with a theoretical knowledge of disability awareness and equality of opportunity. But this awareness of injustice may often be far more keenly honed than the levels of dissatisfaction or frustration expressed by those who are participating as research informants.

Case study research based on the social model of disability has suggested that disability arises as a consequence of a more complex process than being physically, sensorily or mentally impaired and marginalised. Disablement is a process which results from a sequence, or combination, of circumstances and attitudinal judgements. It is suggested that these judgements and opinions come together to form the key features that create a 'lifestyle' and a subjective assessment of one's 'place' in the locality. No one dimension by itself is necessarily deliberate or singly capable of creating marginalisation, but as a total package, or combination, they contribute to an individual's comprehension of his or her place in society. Research activity around the social model also reminds us that it is never possible to identify completely with research informants. Whilst some researchers may become friends with informants, these friendships remain peripheral to the researchers' own lives. Differences of gender, life experience, class and educational background as well as physical and/or sensory impairment influence and shape the structure of interviews, responses and interpretations.

While it may be possible to empathise with an interviewee, informant or research subject, it is impossible to fully comprehend the intricacies and complex psychology of another person's experience. Just as important to consider is the inevitable discomfiture of temporarily 'passing through' another person's life experience. The need to reconcile two worlds is part of the skill of the developing researcher in Disability Studies. Knowing how to move in, however sensitively or intensively, for a brief period and then return to a different series of relationships and affiliations, in a different social world, is both a personal skill to be developed and an issue to be reflected upon.

Part of the intention of disability research is to go beyond exposing the differentials in provision and resource allocation. It is also required to better understand, inform and feed into the exercise of democratic participation around the outcomes of community care. Developing researchers have to become aware of the consultative exercises that have to go on between services and disabled people, e.g. local health authorities and social services. However, for the majority of people research does not touch their lives. The voices that are heard and the people who tend to attend meetings are those from official organisations, and those individuals used to speaking in public. If for no other reason, therefore, research that sets out to report on the circumstances of people's lives continues to be valuable. It restores the balance somewhat; back to the people themselves, their views and their concerns.

Summary

Research in the area of disability has tended to be dominated by quantitative surveys and questionnaires that estimate and measure the functional limitations of people in their day-to-day lives. Such research has served to confirm disability as an individual deficit. It has often been conducted by non-disabled researchers in a fashion that places them outside the circumstances of disabled people and their families. The more recent interest in the development of qualitative, case study, research conducted by disabled people themselves, or in cooperation with non-disabled people, has shifted investigations of disability towards an exploration of the lived experiences of disabled people within the developing policies and practices of inclusive communities.

CHAPTER 8

Medical health and disability

Questions

- What are the implications of health care for people with learning difficulties?
- How can training programmes for health care professionals respond to the particular risk factors associated with the poor health of people with disabilities?
- What would need to be included in a proposal for the development of a 'healthy lifestyle' for people with learning difficulties in your district?
- What are the links between symptoms of illness, isolation and attitudes towards disablement?
- How might *The Health of the Nation* strategies improve the circumstances of people with learning difficulties?

Introduction

We live in a society that values good health, physical fitness and well-being as 'wholeness'. As a society we link ability with physical fitness, power, money and sexuality. Such values tend to sustain and reinforce some fundamental and negative judgements about the value of disabled people. The promotion of the right of people with disabilities to enjoy appropriate health and opportunities for personal relationships is still not universally acclaimed. People are respected more for doing things, for being active rather than being passive and dependent. The idea that those with disabilities might also wish to enjoy sexual relationships as part of a healthy lifestyle has taken even longer to be accepted.

One of the most striking features of the history of disability is the nature and prevalence of impairments and handicapping conditions. One dramatic indicator of the improvement in the health and well-being of children has been the greater life expectancy in the 1990s than a hundred years ago. Diseases such as polio are now virtually non-existent in the United Kingdom and tuberculosis, which killed more than 3,000 people a year at the beginning of the century, is now both rare and easily treatable. Advances in the efficacy of drugs and medicines, combined with improvements in surgical skills, have significantly reduced the incidence of certain medical conditions linked to impairments and disablement. Not only are these changes reflected in the improved survival rates but recovery from many conditions can now be complete, whereas in the past it was only partial. Nevertheless, it is a paradox that while medical skill has significantly reduced the incidence and prevalence of certain deformities, the same skill has enabled increasing numbers of children with severe and profound disabling conditions to survive.

The link between health, social acceptance and the image of the body has always been dangerously ambiguous. To be healthy implies a positive relationship between physical, social and mental states of well-being. This interrelationship between 'healthy lifestyle', environmental factors, exercise and diet has become increasingly relevant in the development of health for all of us. However, for disabled people the 'biological clock' of disablement particularly highlights the link between the medicalisation of impairment, increased longevity and changing patterns of living. Advanced medical knowledge means many people are surviving illnesses that previously would have proved fatal, but which leave them severely disabled. This in turn has a number of implications for the development of rehabilitation and care services and for the training of staff. Similar considerations apply to the effective development of multi-agency services in order to mitigate psychological and emotional distress.

Disability and health

Marris (1996) has argued that there are parallels between the treatment of the female body and the treatment of the health needs of disabled people of both sexes.

> A disabled person's body is one which is acted upon, one which has things done to it because it doesn't function properly. We may experience surgery, tests that involve taking blood or other substances from us, or drug treatment with their side effects . . . . Our ill bodies, like women's bodies are therefore more animal, less sublime, and everyday we are surrounded by images of thin, well, active bodies, with their implicit negative messages about our own bodies, our limited energy levels or physical limitations. (p. 20)

One of the major mistakes so often made in relation to disability is to associate an illness label with an impairment and then to generalise that label. For example, the labels of a 'heart defect' or cerebral palsy are open to a range of interpretations and responses. One person diagnosed with a heart condition may be able to lead a perfectly normal life, another person may be bedridden, while a third may be only capable of limited exercise. The effects of cerebral palsy may be so mild in one person as to be only recognisable to an experienced observer; another person may have enormous difficulty in speaking, eating or walking.

Research also suggests that the health risks faced by people with disabilities are greater than had previously been believed, e.g. cardiovascular disease and cancers appear to be more common and a high proportion of people with disabilities (and particularly learning disabilities) 'carry one or more risk factors associated with morbidity and mortality from these causes' (Turner and Moss 1995, p. 2).

The planning of the delivery of health and medical care for someone who has a disability is also a major issue, particularly as they move from child to adult services. A person with an impairment such as spina bifida or cerebral palsy, whose legs are affected but who has a good mental capacity, may be able to respond better to physiotherapy than another person with cerebral palsy or spina bifida who also has a learning disability and who cannot understand the directions given by the physiotherapist. For the majority of people, the general practitioner is often the first port of call when someone is ill. He or she may be unaware of how to interact with a physically disabled, or learning disabled person; or may believe that more specialised care is required.

It is probable that everyone is born with some kind of health defect. Some people may be slightly pigeon-toed, others may have a mole or birthmark of some kind. These are minor blemishes, non-disabling and normally overlooked until some of them re-emerge as more problematic health issues in later life. However, in the past, birth deformities have been considered both an ancient curse and a mark of status. Images of deformity appear in surviving records of the oldest civilisations. It has been noted that achondroplasia (dwarfism) is illustrated in Egyptian tomb paintings more than five thousand years old.

> Clubfoot was known in the XIth and XIIth dynasties; a cleft palate has been discovered in an Egyptian mummy, and cases of harelip and congenital amputations are recorded in pre-historic Peruvian pottery. Using clay tablets the Babylonians catalogued more than sixty deformities of the ear, nose, mouth and limbs. (Marshall 1976, p. 2)

Birth defects are mistakes in body formation, or function, that can be caused by heredity, disease, or by environmental influences. Heredity and environment may work together to produce a child with a health defect. Such is the extent of human variation that it is impossible to give a precise definition of a birth defect. However, it is generally accepted to be anything that is present at birth that will deprive the child of physical or mental health. Some dysfunctions are so slight that they may be classed as inconveniences, e.g. left-handedness or colour blindness. On the other hand there are birth defects involving many organs which result in rapid and premature death within hours after birth. Between these extremes there are a range of conditions that are medically well known. Diabetes and muscular dystrophy are examples of abnormalities in body chemistry, whilst limb deformities and cleft palates are associated with errors in the anatomical structure of the body. All these conditions are congenital defects, as are some blood disorders such as haemophilia.

A great many birth defects are caused by a combination of heredity and environmental factors working together. Nevertheless, just as heredity can make some individuals and not others react to allergens in the environment (like pollen and some drugs), so a particular unborn child's inherited predisposition in the womb may be influenced when another baby may show no environmental reaction at all. For example, not every woman who has rubella in early pregnancy will give birth to a child with an impairment and not all women in the 1960s who took the drug thalidomide early in their pregnancy gave birth to malformed infants. Subtle genetic influences have probably had a greater impact on us all.

A healthy lifestyle

The health of both populations and individuals is inextricably bound up with economic development. Whilst it is by no means clear that health status automatically improves with rising levels of development, there are clear correlations. Using the United Nations' population statistics for 1990 it is possible to identify a global estimate, for the prevalence of people with moderate and severe disability, of 5.2 per cent (Helander 1993, p. 22). Nevertheless, when it is realised that these estimates refer to prevalence of disability and 'need for rehabilitation' this can be considered to be a global underestimate. The often cited estimate made by the World Health Organisation in 1976, of 10 per cent of the world population, may in fact be nearer to the truth. This estimate was based on a number of calculations of disability rates resulting from diseases, trauma, malnutrition, genetic causes, etc. These calculations included a high proportion of people with slight and reversible disabilities, such as those caused by malnutrition. In any given country, the more it is possible to feed all inhabitants, to provide regular water supply and basic preventative medicine, the less likely is the incidence of severe and long-term disablement.

The prevalence of disablement in the world is estimated to be close to 300 million people. However, this figure does not include temporary or short-term disabilities caused by curable diseases or reversible conditions. Disability has come to be linked with a range of conditions and defects other than purely physical ones. In many cases the main causes of disablement are illnesses and diseases which have a damaging effect on the body. Diabetes, kidney failure, severe asthma are examples. As has already been noted, disablement also arises from wider social factors in a person's life and environment.

Genetic diseases and disability

> Since the dawn of time the human race has been suffering from the consequences of genetic disease. Even now, most of the four thousand or so of the conditions which result from mutations in a single gene remain incurable, blighting the hopes of whole families and casting the long shadow of inherited disorders across generations. (Kent 1996, p. 5)

Biotechnology and genetic medicine hold the keys that may radically transform our concepts of health and disease in the foreseeable future. It is the responsibility of politicians and regulators to create the framework that will facilitate and encourage this in response to the entirely legitimate demands of millions of people in families whose lives are affected by the uncertainties of genetic diseases.

It has been reliably estimated that across the European nations that make up the European Union, as many as 30,000 children die each year as a direct result of genetic disorders. Possibly ten times this number are born with significant impairments or long-term health problems (Kent 1996, p. 73). As examples, both cystic fibrosis and haemophilia are inherited recessive gene disorders. However, as scientific knowledge of human genetics advances, it is clear that more common diseases such as breast cancer, osteoporosis and diabetes have been discovered to have a genetic component. The main characteristics of cystic fibrosis are chronic lung infection, poor digestion due to pancreatic insufficiency and the possibility of liver malfunction in some people. As people with cystic fibrosis grow older they tend to develop a specific form of diabetes. Despite the ever-improving survival rates, and intensive research, it is still the case that cystic fibrosis leads to premature death. Haemophilia, the blood-clotting disease that mainly causes internal bleeding of the knees, elbows and other joints, is also a genetically predetermined condition, although it is probably now best known in relation to the publicity arising from the HIV/ blood transfusion scandals of the 1980s.

Where families are at a known risk of carrying, or are affected by, a genetic disorder the recent rapid advances in scientific understanding of the human genome carry the potential for effective intervention. Research also carries with it the ethical risks associated with any bio-medical enquiry into genetic disease (see Chapter 5).

Chromosomal abnormality

There are a number of syndromes associated with disabling conditions that are a result of chromosomal abnormalities. Down's Syndrome is the most common condition that results from a chromosomal disorder. The condition is characterised by a flatness of the face and thick epicanthal folds around the corners of the eyes, making them appear to slant upwards. Other features include a protruding tongue, defective heart, webbing of the skin folds between fingers and toes, short height and a tendency to obesity. There are basically three types of Down's Syndrome. By far the most common is trisomy 21, where there is an extra chromosome on the 21st pair of chromosomes in the nucleus that becomes a human embryo. In effect, the 21st set of chromosomes is in reality a triplet rather than a pair, causing a condition called trisomy. Mosaicism in cell structure arises because of faulty cell development as a consequence of chromosomal disorders. Some of an individual's cells may have an extra chromosome while others do not and this leads to the condition of Down's Syndrome.

The likelihood of having a child with Down's Syndrome is dependent to a great extent on maternal age. More Down's Syndrome infants tend to be born to women over the age of 40. The medical procedure of amniocentesis, involving examination of the amniotic fluid around the foetus in the uterus, is sometimes recommended to older women in the 18th to 20th week of pregnancy in order to determine whether or not the child will be born with Down's, or other chromosomal abnormality.

Metabolism or nutrition

Most genetically determined impairments are attributed to metabolic disorders. Two such conditions caused by a combination of defective recessive genes are phenylketonuria (PKU) and galactosaemia. PKU involves the inability of the body to convert phenylalanine, a common dietary substance, into tyrosine. The accumulation of phenylalanine results in abnormal brain development and can lead to mental impairment. The condition can be detected by a screening test shortly after birth and controlled by dietary measures throughout childhood. Galactosaemia, another metabolic disorder, is a disease that involves the inability to metabolise galactose and again can be controlled through dietary regulation, e.g. by following a regime of a milk-free diet.

As the interest in nutrition and healthy eating has grown, so the manufacturers of food and dietary supplements have begun to claim that food supplements can act as medicines providing cures or treatment for certain diseases. The Food Commission in surveying over 300 products and their promotional literature has found many claims appearing to border on illegality: 'dozens of cases where manufacturers are making claims which imply the products have a medicinal effect contrary to the Medicines Act. Others are making carefully worded claims which imply a health benefit without expressly making a medical claim' (*The Food Magazine* 1997, p. 1).

Infection and toxicity

There are a number of infections that have a serious effect on foetal development; some affect the mother while others are particular to the developing baby. Rubella, syphilis and herpes simplex in pregnant mothers are all conditions that can cross the placental barrier and lead to impairments and disabilities in the unborn foetus. Rubella can be controlled through preventive vaccination but is most dangerous in the first three months of pregnancy (trimester). The venereal diseases of syphilis and herpes simplex, on the other hand, present a greater risk at later stages of foetal development. Examples of infection in the child rather than the mother are meningitis and encephalitis. Meningitis is an infection of the covering of the brain which may be caused by a variety of bacterial or viral agents. The condition can lead to mental retardation and or sensory impairment. The more serious infection of encephalitis is an inflammation of the brain. It can lead to immediate trauma and mental dysfunction, or the effects may not occur until years later.

Like infections, poisoning can occur in the expectant mother or the unborn child. During the past 20 years there has been a growing awareness of the harmful effects of a variety of substances, e.g. the toxic effects of tobacco, alcohol and even food additives, as well as the more well known hazards of hard drugs such as heroin. The more subtle effects of prescribed drugs have also been implicated as being harmful to the development of the foetus. Less well understood are the potential hazards of environmental pollutants in exhaust fumes, lead based paint and toxic agents which affect organisms at the lower levels of the food chain. The problems of drug abuse are disturbingly widespread in their effect when it is recognised that drug availability is more common than one might at first believe and that drug-poisoning can come in a variety of forms, e.g. cigarettes, alcohol, glue, paint, cold remedies, amphetamines, valium-based products.

Just as drug misuse may have consequences that can lead to impairments, so too can the use of drugs be used as a method of therapy and intervention. The treatment of Attention Deficit Hyperactive Disorder (ADHD) is commonly through prescribed drugs. ADHD is a condition in children and young people, typically characterised by distraction, short memory and physical over-activity. Sufferers are often talkative, have poor concentration and are low in achievement and work output. While there is no consensus on the causes of ADHD, recent theoretical considerations suggest that 'more than 80 per cent of cases are caused by a malfunction within the inner ear system' (Jensen 1995, p. 286). This is the area that affects vision, regulates balance and sensory motor responses. It is a feature of hyperactivity that the most successful treatment for overcoming the learning disabilities arising from the condition is through a prescription of activity-inducing amphetamine-based drugs, such as Ritalin.

Trauma or physical agents

The brain of the developing foetus and young child is relatively vulnerable to a variety of accidents. Damage to the brain can occur before, during or after birth and can lead to impairments. Before birth high levels of X-ray can result in brain dysfunction. Injury can also occur during delivery if the child is not positioned properly in the uterus. A difficulty that can sometimes occur during delivery is anoxia (deprivation of oxygen). After birth, a blow to the head can, of course, cause damage to a child's brain and lead to impaired development of the nervous system.

The health needs of people with disabilities

Studies of the health and lifestyle of people with disabilities have tended to concentrate on the concerns for primary health care of populations in institutions. There is now an accumulation of evidence that changes in longevity and lifestyle as a result of the closures of long-stay hospitals are altering the health-related disorders of people living in non-institutional settings and these changes are being reflected in the death rates of disabled people. Ironically, people with greater independence, living in the community, may now be more likely to follow lifestyles which place a higher risk on their health, resulting in more health-risk related deaths, e.g. from smoking, poor nutrition, and cardiovascular disorders.

There are a number of ways in which living in the community may bring higher health risks. People with disabilities in the United Kingdom are now exposed to many of the increased risk factors relating to cardiovascular disease, cancers, mental illness, sexual health and accidents that affect the rest of society. In addition they face increased risks of obesity and fitness-related factors. These are particular threats for people who may already face a range of other health-related impairments, such as visual and hearing disorders and poor dental health. Obesity has been linked to increased mortality from cancer of the colon, rectum and of the prostate in men. In women it is associated with cancer of the gall bladder, breast, cervix and ovaries (Garrow 1988). These risks affect people equally and apply to the general population at large as well as people with disabilities; however, opportunistic screening would identify more cases at an earlier age and help to prevent the onset of obesity-related disablement.

Screening for osteoporosis, as another example, would benefit not simply older people who suffer from inadequate and discriminatory health care, but more specifically women (who statistically outlive men anyway) who have gone beyond the menopause. Henwood (1990) indicates that there are more than 46,000 people in England and Wales who suffer hip fractures each year and 60 per cent of them are women over the age of 75.

The impact of discrimination in relation to health screening in old age suggests that there are a number of hard decisions to be made. The efficacy of health screening in old age may be more limited than using resources to improve lifestyle in preference to detecting disease. There are a number of erroneous assumptions made about the nature of diseases in older people and response to treatment. There is a relatively high proportion of cancers, gastro-intestinal disorders, foot disorders, balance disorders, incontinence and obesity associated with disabled people in old age. However, the relative under-treatment of, for example, cancer in older people means that tumours which could be controlled or cured are not (Henwood 1990). In addition to Alzheimer's disease and dementia, other conditions associated with early ageing have also been identified among adults with Down's Syndrome. Musculo-skeletal weakness and particular conditions such as osteoporosis have been observed as preventable risk factors: 'osteoporosis fractures in the elderly present a major healthcare and social problem which is largely preventable. The consequences of these fractures are enormous both socio-economically and as regards morbidity and mortality' (Office of Health Economics 1990, p. 19).

The Health of the Nation

The *Health of the Nation* initiative was established by central government in 1992. It established five key national priority areas for improving understanding of the health needs of the population:

- coronary heart disease and stroke
- cancer
- mental illness
- HIV, AIDS and sexual health
- accidents.

In 1995 it was also established that the sub-population of people with learning disabilities should be considered a priority group for considerations of preventative health care (HMSO 1995). It has been particularly evident that the risk factors related to these five areas are at least as prevalent among people with learning difficulties as among the general population. Research into the healthy lifestyles of this sub-population suggests that whilst strategies for health promotion amongst learning-disabled people are encouraged, the most common initiatives tend to be around weight loss/maintenance and healthy eating. There is less consideration given to areas such as fitness, or anti-smoking education (Turner 1996).

Coronary heart disease and stroke

There is evidence that the risk factors associated with cardiovascular disease are at least as prevalent among people with learning difficulties as in the general population (Turner and Moss 1995). Increased risks of cardiovascular disease have been linked with obesity, higher cholesterol levels and hypertension. Studies in both the UK and the USA suggest that obesity is higher among people with learning difficulties than among the general population. Bell and Bhate (1992), in a survey report, indicated that 19 per cent of males and 35 per cent of females living in a community for people with disabilities were found to be obese. These figures compare with 6 per cent and 8 per cent respectively of the general population.

Poor cardiovascular fitness is indicative of a sedentary lifestyle and this tends to be confirmed by the limited number of studies that have been conducted in this area in the United Kingdom. Flynn and Hirst (1992) found that a low proportion of a sample of young people with learning disabilities aged between 14 and 22 took part in sport compared with a matched sample of young people in the general population and that much of their time was spent in passive activities such as watching television.

Cancer

Cancers are the most common causes of death in the UK, after heart disease, and account for approximately 25 per cent of deaths (HMSO 1992). There is some evidence that cancer-related deaths are beginning to increase among the population of people with disabilities. Jancar (1990) found that death rates from cancer in an institution in the UK increased from 10 per cent in the period 1931–80 to 17 per cent of all deaths in the period 1976–85. Jancar concluded that this may indeed be due to increased longevity, but the findings also indicate a significant increase in certain gastro-intestinal cancers, which may be a reflection of certain unexplained changes in lifestyle. As with heart disease, deaths due to cancer appear more prevalent among people with moderate and mild learning disorders than those with more profound and multiple disabilities (O'Brien et al. 1991). There has been a long and well established link between death from leukaemia and Down's Syndrome. This is estimated at between ten and twenty times greater than in the general population (Fong and Brodeur 1987).

Mental illness

Mental illness is the third of the *Health of the Nation* key areas. Evidence from a number of large-scale studies suggests that the prevalence of mental ill health amongst disabled people is somewhat different compared with the general population. The evidence indicates that the prevalence of mental illness in people with learning disabilities is at least as high as in the general population (Moss 1995; Turner and Moss 1995). For a person with a learning disability, whose adaptive skills may already be limited, an additional mental illness is likely to lead to the need for considerable levels of support and a seriously impaired quality of life.

Sexual health

The promotion of the rights of people with learning difficulties to enjoy appropriate health and sex education and opportunities for personal and sexual relationships has been established as a key theme of *The Health of the Nation*. It recommends a strategy that seeks to reduce the incidence of HIV and other sexually transmitted diseases and encourages the development of effective family planning services. There is a huge range of information available concerning the need for 'safe sex' to prevent sexually transmitted diseases. Unfortunately, this information is not always easily accessible to people with disabilities (Shakespeare et al. 1996, p. 17). There is an assumption that disabled people, particularly those with a learning difficulty, have limited sexual activity. In fact, the idea that people with learning difficulties might wish to enjoy permanent sexual relationships and marriage is still treated as a taboo subject which is both unclear and contradictory in its messages for disabled people. For example, whilst it is not illegal to carry out a sexual act with a woman who is learning disabled, provided she has given consent, two people with learning-difficulties wishing to marry are still expected to seek consent for their actions from a professional member of the caring services.

An important aspect of sexual health, particularly for people with learning difficulties, is the detection and prevention of sexual abuse. This applies to people living in the community as much as to those remaining in institutions. In recent years the extent of physical and sexual abuse experienced by people with disabilities has become more widely known and discussed. Harassment and abuse is offensive and an obscene violation of anyone who is a victim. However, for people with disabilities the offence is amplified by their relative powerlessness as victims of attack. In order to counter this, a number of strategies have been developed. For example, British Telecom have established a separate specialised mini-com (text phone) line to monitor harassment arising from sexually obscene or malicious telephone messages to deaf people (Disability Now 1996, p. 6).

Nowadays the risk of people with learning difficulties being sexually abused is an acknowledged, if sad, fact of life. The issue of sexual abuse with its additional hazards of HIV and other sexually transmitted diseases, or psychological damage, has been studied by Turk and Brown (1993) in residential settings in the UK. They indicate that the risk of abuse comes almost equally from other residents, from staff, family members and others. Turk and Brown also report that 55 per cent of the 119 cases studied allegedly resulted in emotional trauma for the victim.

Accidents

Accidents are the most common cause of death among people under 30 in the general population. The majority of these occur on the roads or in the home. An aim to reduce the incidence of accidents is the fifth of the *Health of the Nation* key areas.

Although the use of a car is likely to be much lower amongst disabled people, there is some evidence that fatal accidents may be more common amongst people with learning difficulties. *The Health of the Nation* refers to people with disabilities having an increased vulnerability to accidents and, thereby, requiring the involvement of carers and services, including the provision of safety items and adaptations (HMSO 1992, pp. 113–14). This increased risk relates to the high prevalence of certain conditions (e.g. dementia among older people with Down's Syndrome, vision loss, movement disorders and skeletal abnormalities). It has been speculated that particular conditions that are vulnerable to accident, such as the high prevalence of atlantoaxial vertebra instability among children with Down's Syndrome, may be linked to the high incidence of degenerative arthritis of the neck among adults (Howells 1989).

The need for recreation, pastimes and relaxation

There has been very little published research in relation to exercise, fitness, diet and weight loss amongst disabled people in the United Kingdom. Research evaluating weight loss programmes amongst people with disabilities in the United States generally reveals patchy results. Studies concerned with the maintenance of weight loss are particularly unconvincing, reporting that some subjects in a small-scale study actually gained weight in the 12 months following the baseline measurement (Fox *et al.* 1984). It is probable that neither diet nor exercise, by themselves, will be sufficient for long-term maintenance of weight loss and what will be required are intervention programmes that can be sustained and monitored at regular intervals.

Access to recreational facilities and to recreation itself is, literally, a vital component for everyone. Recreation embraces a complete range of different pastimes. It is a way friendships are formed outside the workplace or home environment; it can also be a way to keep fit. The physiological and emotional needs that can be met from recreational pursuits are vital to a balanced, healthy lifestyle and include enjoyment, competition and satisfaction.

Alternative and complementary medicine

Many disabled people who have experienced years of surgery in childhood feel that the medical profession creates as many difficulties as it cures. As market economics have begun to create internalised competition within state-run health services in a number of countries, the funding of provision formerly freely available to all people is coming under threat. Changes in the funding of the National Health Service are particularly worrying for people whose impairment is also a serious illness. As the long-term costs for care and medical provision become increasingly the responsibility of individuals, the additional expenses of people with disabilities compared to non-disabled people places upon them a disproportionate financial burden.

For some disabled people, therapies such as acupuncture, homoeopathy, aromatherapy and diet have provided an alternative or antidote to conventional medicine. As Marris (1996) has suggested, a holistic approach is fundamental to most complementary therapies. The emphasis is on treating the whole person rather than individual organs or parts of the body. A holistic philosophy also guides the spirit of anthroposophy that underlies the teaching of Rudolf Steiner, whose first requirement is that those who follow his principles should turn their attention to the improvement of their physical and mental or spiritual health (Steiner 1994).

Marris (1996) argues that complementary medicine can offer a radical challenge to the inclination for victim-blaming. The holistic approach offers the possibility of a more equal relationship between practitioner and patient; it recognises and appreciates that health care involves an appreciation of the multiple stresses on both individuals and the environment in which they live. Complementary and holistic medicine does, nevertheless, have its own limitations, the most obvious being availability and expense. She also raises other criticisms:

> Just as with conventional preventive medicine, we are given a set of rules to live by, such as avoiding alcohol, cigarettes and various kinds of food. Once again the blame for illness can be laid on our shoulders if we do not do the right things. The much clearer understanding that exists within complementary medicine of the links between physical and mental well-being can also lead to undue pressure to think positively all the time. It becomes a duty to have our emotional house completely in order. (Marris 1996, p. 201)

Summary

Illness can be a solitary experience. Something as minor as a cold, or a toothache, can make people feel excluded and cut off. The experience of living with an illness in a culture which does not have high regard for people who are ill or disabled has influenced the way in which people think about their world, their politics and their health. The health of people with disabilities is particularly linked to strategies for prevention and rehabilitation. Thus, The Health of the Nation has identified five key areas that have reference to people with learning difficulties. They also suggest that the whole population is increasingly being expected to take more responsibility for their own health and exercise needs and the preventative strategies which can help to ward off ill health. It is no longer sufficient to believe that the state will meet the costs of treatment. Research findings also suggest that people with learning difficulties, who are now living in the community, are more vulnerable to the health risks associated with daily living (e.g. heart attack, stress, obesity) than their counterparts in institutions. This is a marker of an inclusive lifestyle that is perhaps more unintended than anticipated.

The marginalisation of disabled people both in health maintenance, disease prevention, lifestyle and in their interaction with wider society has a variety of causes. Urban areas, housing, sports, leisure and health facilities are designed by people with an idealised imagination and a conviction that tends to preclude the participation of all. The majority of the population are bound by the designs and convictions of a minority. Some of these issues serve as the basis for Chapter 9.

The enabling environment

Questions

- Consider the environmental barriers for people with physical impairments in the normal household. How might they be overcome?
- What are the limitations of technology in overcoming communication difficulties?
- Contact your local or regional resource centre for adaptive aids. How do they assess and match people with the equipment available?

Introduction

There are a variety of personal, environmental and architectural barriers that can prevent the full participation of disabled people in society. There is still a great deal of work to be done if disabled people are to become central to the removal of these obstacles. The chapter will focus upon three key areas:

- Physical and technological environments (housing, transport systems and access to public amenities and information technology).
- Social and recreational environments (including opportunities for participation by disabled people in the planning and delivery of services).
- Economic environments (which includes employment, and access to income and financial benefits).

The census surveys of disabled people (Martin, Meltzer et al. 1988) suggest that some 4.3 million people in the United Kingdom cannot walk for a quarter of a mile without stopping and/or without severe discomfort, and that 2.3 million people cannot stand alone without severe discomfort. These are two of the bald facts that maintain the image of dependency that is associated with impairment and disability. And from behind these utilitarian statistics has emerged a growing industry of technological aids and equipment intended to facilitate the lives and circumstances of disabled people. The rehabilitation industry of care management includes access to increasingly sophisticated prostheses, mobility aids and other items of equipment intended to provide a more enabling experience.

The socio-political structures that have shaped both the practical and aesthetic space of the built environment have remained largely under-researched in relation to disabled people. However, creating barrier-free environments for people with a range of impairments is about more than examining the physical dimensions of buildings. Doors, ramps and lifts are all undeniably important in making the built environment more accessible, but as Napolitano (1996) has indicated, good inclusive design is also about psychological dimensions of change. Disabled people can be given positive messages when the front entrances of buildings are ramped, or transport systems and the signing on notices are sensitively worded, at the right height and clearly visible:

> The element of struggle so often present in daily life fades, confidence and the ability to function is enhanced and a relaxed and open attitude is more likely to prevail. When making access arrangements this psychological element needs to be considered carefully: if the way that disabled people are expected to get into buildings is round the back, past the bins and through the kitchens, what message does that communicate? (Napolitano 1996, p. 33)

Physical, social and recreational environments

Discrimination against disabled people is most noticeably visible and blatant when related to access to buildings and transport. There are numerous studies which have highlighted the combination of patronisation and discrimination that maintains the physical exclusion of the majority of disabled people (e.g. Flynn 1989; Gooding 1994; Morris 1991, 1996; Bynoe et al. 1991; Imrie 1996). Imrie has commented that most modernist architectural ideals continue to be fundamentally ablist:

> In particular, it is popularly assumed that because the built environment seems to facilitate access for the majority of the population (which is a contestable notion), it is the responsibility of the minority to cope by overcoming their handicaps and/or compensating for them. (Imrie 1996, p. 12)

By promoting the social model of disablement, people with disabilities have started to reconceptualise and transform the worlds that we all share and inhabit: 'the emergence of direct action is, in part, premised on an assertion of their differences and on critiques of state welfarism and the paternalism of the wider structures of the "caring" industries' (Imrie 1996, p. 166). This politicisation of the distinctions between 'ablist' space and 'disablist' space, mainly as a result of action by disabled people and their organisations, has begun to highlight the often blatant discrimination and oppression that has subordinated disabled people. Morris (1993) has, for example, illustrated the way in which choice in housing patterns for disabled people has been restricted in terms of both geographical location and architectural design.

Legislation relating to the built environment and disabled people tends still to be more adequately met in the conditions of the 1970 Chronically Sick and Disabled Persons Act than the Disability Discrimination Act 1995. This latter piece of enabling legislation has no powers to enforce compliance and carries a substantial number of clauses that permit avoidance of full legal compliance. The main regulatory provision with regards to disabled people that reflects government policy for the pursuit of merely utilitarian ideals is Part M of Schedule 1 of the Building Regulations. This is a piece of building law that requires access and facilities for disabled people to be provided in certain classes of new buildings. (See Imrie 1996, pp. 101 and 117–18 for further details.) As Chapter 3 has indicated, the section of the legislation on employ-ment does not apply to firms with less than 20 employees. This means that some '96 per cent of Britain's employers are not affected by the new law' when it comes to the requirement to make adaptations to access in the workplace (Barnes 1996).

Much of the built environment – housing, transport, public buildings and amenities, including places of worship – remains inaccessible to disabled people. There is a general view among the leisure industry, as Barnes (1996) points out, that the presence of disabled people in cinemas, pubs, clubs, restaurants and other places of public togetherness is bad for business. Images of disabled people in the communication media also continue to present a particularly horrid and distorted view of the experiences of disability and impairment.

One of the ways in which attempts to create enabling environments go badly wrong is when in removing one barrier another is created. This is a common dilemma for people with mobility impairments who wish to have access to the few adapted toilets that exist for disabled people. Often the lava-tories are kept permanently locked or are inaccessible without assistance. One author highlights the issue:

> Whether the mobility impaired person is stopping off at a motorway ser-
> vice station or a public convenience they will be confronted by the same
> thing. While non-disabled people can simply walk into a lavatory, or get in
> for a small price, people with mobility impairments have to send off search
> parties for someone who has a key . . . . (Napolitano 1996, p. 31)

Another concern emerges when good and reasonable access has been
developed and incorporated into an existing building, but non-disabled
people simply abuse or use the facility insensitively. For example, think of
the number of lavatories for disabled people that are misused as store cup-
boards, with mops and buckets, lightbulbs removed or furniture placed too
close to the doors for the facility to be accessible to somebody in a wheel-
chair; think too of the vehicles parked across ramped entrances to buildings,
preventing people with mobility impairments from leaving or entering.

For everyone there is the need to relax from life's everyday responsibilities
and roles (e.g. to drop in to the local pub for a drink with friends at Sunday
lunchtime, to go for a walk in the country, to share an intimate meal or play a
game of football). These are but a few examples of the ways in which people
relax and spend their leisure time.

As Chapter 8 indicated, access to recreational facilities and to recreation itself is a vital component of everyone's health. It should be remembered that
whilst our concentration is upon the demands for accessible recreation from
disabled people, there are many who are unable to take advantage of sport
and recreation. For a variety of reasons the single parent on welfare benefits
is isolated from recreation as a consequence of his or her poverty and environmental conditions; the solitary individual who feels that they cannot
participate in social activities becomes the social isolate; and the executives
who leave no time in their lives for activities other than their work lead themselves to stress and isolation within their families.

If access to relaxation is denied or made difficult then access to the complete
satisfaction of a whole range of human needs is also denied. Exclusion can
emerge from the physical limitations of a venue (such as a cinema with limited
wheelchair access). It can also emerge as a result of ignorance and prejudice,
e.g. the belief that someone with a disability is not interested in many
recreational activities, or is unable to participate in them. There is also a long-
standing belief that presumes that people with disabilities should go to special
clubs or venues and be offered activities like tray-making or wicker basket
weaving. Worthy pastimes as they are, they should not remain the sole
relaxations available to disabled people!

There is a convenient tradition of service-dependency and a consequent
limitation of choice offered to disabled people. This has tended to allow non-
disabled people in society to feel 'comfortable' with the issue of disability and

at the same time allowed them to ignore the full range of human diversity and potential in relation to the rights of disabled people to take part in recreational activity whether organised or informal. Ironically, the comparative lack of competitive success of British athletes in the 1996 Olympic Games has escalated the profile of the para-Olympic movement and has made disabled sport more visible. These top class athletes are seen increasingly as top class athletes who have a disability and not as disabled athletes. The role that these athletes play is of great importance as they are grabbing the attention of a society that admires competition and forcing the issue of disability to be heard. Disabled people are seen not only as capable of enjoying sport but as extremely competitive, excellent sports people. This can only have a positive effect on the development of a fuller range of recreational activity for all people who have a disability.

Housing

Having a decent home, possessions and comforts is important to our physical and material well-being and our planning for the future. However, where we live depends on a number of factors, not least of which is level of income. It is difficult to measure, but not difficult to imagine the impact of inappropriately adapted housing on the lives of physically impaired people. There are over four million people with mobility impairments in the United Kingdom and there are only 80,000 accessible homes.

It is transparently obvious that the majority of housing stock is unsuitable for people with mobility impairments. However, the main area of social inequality in relation to housing arises from social divisions. The housing inequalities of disabled people are evident from the incidence of homelessness amongst disabled people in the population. This arises as a consequence of low earnings potential and as a consequence of the heavy reliance placed upon the rented sector of the housing market at a time when there are fewer houses available for rent. The lack of purpose-built or adapted housing for disabled people has also helped to increase the numbers of disabled people who are homeless (Morris and Winn 1993).

The concept of accessible housing would mean that thresholds would be level, doorways sufficiently wide and electric sockets at reasonable heights. The essential features within kitchens, bathrooms and toilets would be placed with more thought and consideration for everybody's needs. Thus, they would be within the reach of independent access. At the moment, equipment and fittings are not immediately suitable for the majority of people (e.g. the elderly, children and certainly not for people with mobility impairments).

As access groups throughout the United Kingdom have observed, houses are used by a succession of occupants over different periods of their life cycles and should be more suited to these changing circumstances. Gooding (1994) has made the fundamental point that more adaptable housing would not only help to break the mould of the ghettoised selfishness of 'special needs' housing for the disabled minority. It would also help to build a friendlier environment that benefits a wide variety of people. This would encourage more chances to create more humane spaces in which disabled people can entertain others or accommodate friends.

Technology and its limitations

It is evident from the rapid growth in technological aids in every phase of modern living that Information and Communication Technology (ICT) is one of the major influences for improving access, as well as employment and education for disabled people. Participation in community activity from which disabled people were previously excluded has also been assisted by micro-electronic prosthetics, or artificial technical aids. By the beginning of the next century, ICT is likely to be at the heart of the development of independent living and learning.

Having to make do is a common problem for disabled people. Media designed for non-disabled people cannot always be adapted for those with disabilities. An illustration of this can be made with reference to people who are visually impaired and the development of ever-increasing software from Microsoft. Although Microsoft Windows software accounts for 80 per cent of the software market, the system was originally inaccessible to visually impaired people. In similar fashion, disabled people who use computer speech output systems to provide them with textual information may find it uncomfortable to read from their computer screens for long periods of time. The flexibility of a book or a paper text is unavailable to them, replaced instead by the linear time-based format of a computerised speech output. No matter what sort of electronic or technological equipment is available, it is only ever as good as the human support that lies behind it. Technology, of itself, is only one piece of the jigsaw.

Enabling technology has a number of applications for disabled people and focuses on four main areas:

- facilitating communication, e.g. through word processing, voice output communication aids, text to Braille;
- easing the pressure, e.g. having easy access to a computer and relevant

software helping to improve opportunities for accessing libraries, meeting deadlines, paying bills;

- access to mainstream electronic resources, e.g. finding information and communicating with people at the computer, the Internet, CD-ROMs and multi-media;
- use in a diagnostic, restorative or remedial role.

Access to a vast range of information can be achieved through the power of the computer. Just as software packages can be purchased to aid speech development or improve literacy difficulties, access to the Internet can help disabled people participate in discussion groups without having to physically visit them. For example, by using the World Wide Web, or e-mail, people with disabilities can obtain information in exactly the same fashion as any other user, but in an environment which is suited to their physical needs and by using whatever enabling technologies they require.

In relation to the increased independence of disabled people, innovative adaptations and developments are exploiting the power of ICT (e.g. micro-electronics are already being used to help to overcome the handicapping effects of physical and sensory impairments). Opportunities for the development of physical mobility are also enhanced by advances in the improved design of aids and equipment in both the workplace and community settings. These can include such environmental items as remote control devices for opening and shutting doors and improvements in overall standards of access to buildings and work spaces.

The development of micro-electronic technology plays a significant role in the education of children and students with learning difficulties (Warwick *et al.* 1997):

- At a *micro* level the support provided can take the form of advising individuals. ICT can give instructions, coach teachers, provide advice about software and hardware.
- At a *meso* level the ICT can provide opportunities for the exchange of ideas, consultation and developing policy for particular strategies and or techniques (e.g. working groups for the development of ICT for specific handicaps, such as CONVIG for the visually handicapped in the Netherlands and the Marconi Project in the Bologna district of Italy).
- At a *macro* level there are opportunities for national consultation (e.g. in the United Kingdom there is the National Federation of Access Centres which can provide consultancy and diagnostic screening).

Advances in communication technology have begun to make it easier for people with sensory disabilities to attend ordinary social and work settings.

Visual display units attached to voice-sensitive switches have begun to revolutionise communication for those who are physically disabled with a speech defect, with partial hearing or who are deaf. Optical scanning devices such as the Arkenstone Scanner or the Kurtzweil Reading Edge, linked to Braille printers and voice synthesisers, have begun to benefit readers who are partially sighted. Moreover, where once such equipment was considered prohibitively expensive, it has now fallen to a price that makes the purchase not only viable but an important dimension of any support strategy.

Johnstone (1995) has pointed out that the past decade has shown that people with disabilities and children with special needs now expect to have a right to access both the curriculum and opportunities for social independence as a result of advances in micro-electronics and information technology. Difficulties in note-taking, personal record-keeping and drafting written work can now be surmounted through the use of new technology. These advances have played their part in the development of access to equality of educational opportunities.

Although many disabled people have benefited from using information technology, these benefits are neither universal nor fully realised. Vincent (1993) has suggested that this is due to lack of appropriate support beyond the mere provision of equipment and devices. The first line of development for this appropriate support is in assessment of individual needs in relation to the technology available. Simply having access to a computer does not guarantee the development of independent learning or of educational opportunity. Other frustrations with the use of micro-computers have emerged as a result of the limitations in available software. Where the hardware of machinery, speed of loading and amounts of memory have improved dramatically 'much of the available software is, for all its quantity, educationally inadequate' (Hegarty 1993, p. 194). Many of the available programs seem to offer little that could not be achieved as well by other means and without the accompanying frustrations. In other words, much of the available resource material is packaged in a fashion that fails to exploit the potential of the micro-computer or take into account theories of learning.

Support for the development of ICT skills

Interesting examples of the use of computer technology in the United Kingdom are cited in Hawkridge and Vincent (1992) and Vincent (1990). Their studies indicate the value of developing expertise and experience in conjunction with research organisations (e.g. the National Federation of Access Centres), in order to develop both wider networks and disabled people's self-confidence. They indicate how, through the use of appropriate programs, schools and colleges of FE have facilitated the mastery of social and life skills with young learners who have specific learning difficulties. It is clear that this collaboration with regional and national resource centres for the development of both software and hardware (e.g. tracker balls and adapted keyboards) has enabled learners to engage in activities which they consider to be not only appropriate for their age, but also on a par with those activities they see being undertaken by 'mainstream' learners.

The study by Hawkridge and Vincent (1992) reporting their research within the OECD programme for 'Supporting Active Life for Young People with Disabilities' has, nevertheless, pointed to some important reminders about the strengths and limitations of computers for staff and students alike. They suggest that new technology can give students and young people with disabilities and special educational needs both a wider choice of courses and enhanced educational and employment opportunities. While this is broadly true for all aspects of disability and special educational needs, the new technology cannot provide enablement, access or opportunities without a proper assessment and reassessment of an individual's needs, or the appropriate training for students and their teachers and carers, information, advice and technical services.

Providing the technology and assessing and training people to use it are complex activities. Schools, colleges and community education centres need to play a role in the development of work with disabled people and to provide advice, experience and good practice. People will then have opportunities that, in turn, can increase their independence. The new technology can enable people with disabilities and special needs to acquire skills that match current and future requirements in employment. Many employers are still unaware of this.

It may be considered impressive that a severely disabled person can learn to operate a switch with the blink of an eyelid and as a result communicate through a computer. But it requires the sensitive involvement of specialist assessors to determine if this is all that is required to sustain or improve their quality of life. It may be that the interface with a keyboard could be improved by using another part of the body to operate a switch, or that a speech synthesiser could improve communication or even that the position of the equipment could be determined in a more ergonomically efficient fashion. 'The difference between non-assessment and assessment can be the difference between frustration and the benefits of an enabling technology that opens up new opportunities' (Vincent 1993, p. 2).

The immense storage and interactive power of CD-ROM technology, the portability of computers and the growing panoply of technical aids suggests that it is only a matter of time before they can be used by people who wish to study in their own time and yet remain in regular touch with a 'home base'. Electronic tutorials, advice and consultancy via the Internet and arrangements with a specialist tutor or advisor working from a modem-linked computer terminal some distance away in a college, school or resource centre are clearly worth consideration.

The rapidly developing power of ICT emphasises the importance of the personnel who manage it. At present there is no clear professional profile for these professionals who are leading the way. The hardware will be only as effective as the strengths of those who manage its use. Their skills will have to be recognised and rewarded. This potential of ICT also gives rise to an ethical question, concerning the relationship between an 'independent consultant' and the commercial companies with which he or she is in regular contact. Whether it is possible for a consultant to remain completely independent is a matter for debate. It may be more appropriate to establish some professional regulations and set conditions for collaboration.

Benefits and finance as enabling factors

The poor financial circumstances of many disabled people can often be significantly more problematic than the actual impairment that contributes to disablement. The additional costs associated with being disabled can cause a range of competing and contradictory emotions. As the emphasis for long-term care has shifted relentlessly from the responsibility of the state towards the individual, benefits may have begun to be considered as a privilege or charity handout. However, the specific benefits available to disabled people are there as a right to meet the costs of living with a disability, costs such as heating, transport, clothing and personal assistance.

The Social Security system is notoriously complex and for this reason it is best to seek more detailed and specific advice from specialist sources such as the local office of the Benefits Agency or the national welfare handbooks provided by the Child Poverty Action Group. A well-known and regularly updated directory of information and opportunities for disabled people is provided in conjunction with the Royal Association for Disability and Rehabilitation (Darnborough and Kinrade 1996). Benefits paid out to people with disabilities can be either means tested or non-means tested benefits. Means tested benefits are only paid out if people have limited income and capital; they are only awarded following a thorough investigation into people's financial circumstances. The most important means tested sources of benefit are:

- Income Support if you are not in full-time employment;
- Family Credit if you are in full-time employment;
- Disability Working Allowance if you are in full-time work;
- Housing Benefit and Council Tax Benefit whether or not you are in full-time work.

Income Support. This is the main benefit for people with a low income. For people with a disability the general rules for entitlement to Income Support, among them being available for work, may not apply as a direct result of illness or a physical/mental impairment.

Family Credit. Family Credit is unavailable if the level of capital a person has is above a certain amount. It is a weekly payment, normally payable for a period of up to 26 weeks, and it is only payable if a claimant has at least one dependent child. If a disabled person or his or her partner is in receipt of the Disability Working Allowance they will not be entitled to claim Family Credit.

Disability Working Allowance. This is a benefit paid to people who are in work but have a disability which puts them at a disadvantage in the labour market. It tops up a claimant's wages if they are in full-time work. Part-time workers can claim Income Support instead. To qualify for DWA a person must have a disability that puts them at a disadvantage in getting a job.

Housing Benefit. Payable to people on a low income and living in rented property, this can include private and local authority accommodation, including sheltered accommodation. It is not, however, usually available to people in residential care or a nursing home. The amount of benefit received depends on a person's level of income, the number of people in the 'family' and the amount calculated as 'eligible' rent for the purposes of a rebate or allowance.

Non-means tested benefits do not involve a detailed examination of personal finances. So long as a person meets certain basic conditions, called 'conditions of entitlement' (such as being disabled, widowed or available for work), the benefits are payable. Non-means tested benefits are intended to supplement or compensate for inability to work, or any loss of earnings. Thus, for people with disabilities the most significant long-term non-contributory benefits are:

- Severe Disablement Allowance
- Disability Living Allowance
- Attendance Allowance (for people over the age of 65).

Severe Disablement Allowance. A tax-free benefit for people who have been incapable of work for 28 weeks but have not paid enough National Insurance contributions to claim either sickness or invalidity benefits. The lowest age limit is 16 and it is not income-related. People who become disabled after the age of 65 cannot normally claim this benefit.

Disability Living Allowance. A tax-free benefit for people who need help with personal care and/or getting around. The claimant must be under 66 when an application is made and have become disabled before their 65th birthday. The allowance is made up from two parts: a mobility component which has two rates, and a care component which has three. In 1992 this benefit replaced Mobility Allowance and Attendance Allowance for people under the age of 65.

Attendance Allowance. A tax-free allowance that is available to adults who are 65 or over with severe physical or mental disabilities and who require a lot of care or supervision either by day, or by night, or both.

Other sources of help can come from special funds and from local and national charities. The best-known is perhaps the Family Fund, administered by the Joseph Rowntree Memorial Trust. It exists to provide help in the form of goods, services or a grant of money to the families of children under the age of 16 with severe disabilities. The fund has wide discretion to provide help that will relieve stress arising from the day-to-day care of the child. In general, it can only help with certain needs which are not met by statutory services. The following are some examples of the kind of help it has been able to provide:

- hire cars, taxi fares, cars and driving lessons so that a family can go on outings;
- washing machines and dryers;
- clothing, bedding and furnishings;
- in certain circumstances, aids and adaptations;
- family holidays;
- recreation equipment.

A special trust established and financed by the government – the Independent Living Fund – still operates to provide assistance to people with very severe physical or mental disabilities who are on a low income. In 1993 a more restrictive set of rules were set down as criteria for accessing the fund. People who are eligible must be aged between 16 and 65, in receipt of the highest rate of Disability Living Allowance, be living alone or with people who cannot meet the claimant's care needs in full, and be on a low income. The fund is operated through contact and assessment from local Social Services.

Services at home

Social Services departments have a duty to provide certain services to disabled people and to inform disabled people about these services. The Chronically

Sick and Disabled Persons Act 1973 set out the following key services as fundamental, although all are dependent upon a needs assessment from the Social Services.

Home carers. Formerly home helps would visit on a reasonably regular basis to carry out certain tasks. Previously these were domestic tasks, such as cleaning and shopping, but now priority is given to people who need help with personal care such as dressing, toileting and washing.

Meals on wheels. This is a delivery service bringing meals to older and disabled people who cannot leave the house. Vegetarian and special dietary and religious requirements should usually be catered for.

Day centre and respite care. These facilities differ from area to area, but local authorities have a duty to provide or arrange these if a disabled person has been assessed as needing them.

It is becoming increasingly common to find that local authorities are either making a charge for some or all of the above services, or challenging the ruling that they have the responsibility. Although there is still a legal duty to provide services, it is also recognised that the level of service provision is dependent upon the funds available to provide them.

Health services. The family doctor is normally the first point of contact with the health services. GPs can give direct treatment or refer the patient to other parts of the service (e.g. hospital specialists or district nurse). Getting to hospital, for example, can be considered an entitlement for ambulance transportation if a GP considers a patient to be medically unfit to travel to hospital by other means. The costs of travelling to hospital can also be subsidised if someone is in receipt of Income Support or Family Credit.

Other NHS services include district nurses, community occupational therapists, chiropody and special beds for disabled people at home. The NHS also provides an incontinence supply service on referral from a GP or the Social Services Department.

Summary

Attempts to ensure that environmental conditions are accessible to disabled people can often produce adaptations that are insensitive. Architectural aesthetics and health have long been associated with psychological well-being and this is exacerbated by fears of disability and loss. What have been more widely overlooked are other environmental considerations, including levels of disability-related benefits, adaptations in the home and means of assisted communication. Ultimately, students of Disability Studies must develop improved awareness of information technology. This can include updating on the use of the technology for meeting individual needs. However, ICT has exciting possibilities for innovative access to staff development as a whole. This should include the expertise and experience of all participants.

CHAPTER 10

Future directions

Questions

- How should society respond to freedom as power and freedom as right in relation to disabled people?
- Will the search for individual self-determination and choice by disabled people simply reduce diversity and narrow the options available?
- Will the development of Disability Studies, as an academic discipline, prevent the development of inclusive communities?
- How far does the study of disability issues provide an opportunity for the relocation of the professional management of services for disabled people by disabled people?
- How can non-disabled people begin to look at the special oppressions experienced by disabled people without appearing to be tokenistic?

Introduction

In this chapter the issues of rights and entitlements will be readdressed in the light of the advancing acceptance of Disability Studies as an academic discipline. The understanding that disablement is a cultural phenomenon is now well established, and the strength of a disability 'movement' and disabled people themselves as the engine for change is beginning to be understood. However, what has not yet been clearly articulated is the direction that the disability movement is taking. Whilst the relationship between disability politics and the power brokers in the rest of the world is becoming more clearly established, the silent majority of disabled people remain isolated and uninformed. Proposals for the recognition of the rights of disabled people now need to be matched with policies for ensuring that the hard-fought battles for recognition and disability awareness are sustained, and articulated on behalf of all disabled people. Disability Studies as an academic programme has a responsibility to track and evaluate these developments. However, if the study of disability issues remains esoteric and academic, safely placed within higher education, it is in danger of losing some of its essence. The location of Disability Studies within the wider dimensions of community may help to shape change. A more practical, hands-on understanding of services (e.g. the way in which bureaucratic procedures can control both claimants and officers in the distribution of benefits) needs to be developed for a true understanding of power. For Coleridge, the use and abuse of power in the development of alternative service provisions is fundamental to the development of social justice for disabled people: 'the question of how power is handled once it is acquired is as important for the disability movement as for any other liberation movement' (Coleridge 1993, p. 212).

The central task of Disability Studies is to promote the exploration of community values using the perspectives of disabled people. As such the shape of the discipline is closely aligned with the work of the emerging disability movement and the examination of society through an exploration of groups and individuals who are placed at the margins. Through highlighting the denial of citizenship rights and social justice for individuals with disabilities, the disability movement has offered a valuable starting point for the critical evaluation of society. However, as Shakespeare and Watson remind us, such an ideological framing of Disability Studies is only properly located within British disability politics: 'the movement in other countries, while adopting a social minority group approach, have not built their campaign and self-definition around the social model' (Shakespeare and Watson 1997, p. 293).

Over the last two decades, working parties consisting of individuals and groups working on behalf of disabled people have produced reports which have attempted to establish structural social changes intended to remove the final vestiges of those physical, economic or social restrictions that have acted as barriers to the full inclusion of disabled people in mainstream society (e.g. Snowdon 1979, Warnock 1978 and DHSS 1988). However, the recommendations of these reports have tended to reinforce and perpetuate the tradition of marking out disabled people as different and special. As this text has attempted to explain: 'Special is usually synonymous with segregated. Disabled people do not have special needs. We have the same needs as anyone else: basic needs such as information, housing, transport. Disabled people are only abnormal because our ordinary needs are not normally met' (Shakespeare 1997, p. 9).

Approaches to the care and education of disabled people have had the effect of reminding us all that barriers and restrictions are not new and that their removal has been addressed before. The real starting point for their removal lies not solely in legislative change but in the recognition that disability is not simply a personal or individual problem. It is also a collective concern that challenges the underlying structures and principles of social justice, equality, inclusion and autonomous decision making.

Equal rights and entitlements

An important characteristic of the change that has taken place in the disability movement has been the shift towards self-organisation and the taking of control by disabled people themselves in the organisations representing their interests. This has been argued by Oliver (1990) and Fagan and Lee (1997) who remind us that an organisation *of* disabled people (e.g. the British Council of Disabled People or BCODP) has a very different relationship to the state and the political system from an organisation *for* disabled people (e.g. the Royal Association for Disability and Rehabilitation or RADAR). At a wider level, there is a growing recognition in British society that disability is not a matter of certain individuals being unable to meet the demands of society, but of the failure of society to recognise its own disabling potential and our collective failure to address the specific needs that arise from this.

The history of the development of Disability Studies is littered with expressions and descriptions of the public appetite for exhibitions of human freaks and oddities. Thirty years ago, Haffter (1968) in researching the literature into European folklore concerning disabled people remind us that in Tudor and Stuart England a considerable element of popular humour was directed at the eccentric and the deviant, but as middle-class values and Puritan reticence brought changes in public attitudes to 'unavoidable misfortune' it came to be considered inappropriate that disabled people and disability issues should be seen as subjects for humour outside the circuses and travelling freak-shows. For some commentators, these accounts arouse conflicting emotions which are illustrative of the revolution in public attitudes towards disabled people. For Thomas (1978, p. 145) there is 'revulsion at the Roman Holiday mentality that could turn deformity into a commercial venture, and admiration for the human curiosities that fashioned a worthwhile life for themselves in the tolerant and accepting community of the circus'. The status of disabled people has altered from being despised and discriminated against to being derogated through custodial and philanthropic concern and on towards inclusion and self-confidence.

Legislation may have begun to force change in the health, housing, employment and care of disabled people. At the same time this has been accompanied by a growing involvement in the expression of concern from those wishing to help disabled people, either as individuals or through voluntary groups. Much of this help comes from non-disabled men and women and the philanthropic motive still drives many people into volunteering to help:

> They do not wish to play the out-dated Lady Bountiful, but find in their involvement an opportunity to express a concern for human values. Disablement allows some of them to be politically active in an area untouched by ideologies of the extreme right or left. (Thomas 1978, p. 146)

This may still be true, but what is certain, 20 years on, is that the study of disability has become both more radical and more political and that disabled people themselves have become more self-confident in asserting their own interests. This is encapsulated in an acerbic correspondence from one of the 'founding fathers' of the disability movement, commenting on the growing interest in disability by non-disabled people:

> There's something beautifully ironical about an able-bodied person residing in a Western industrial society, who has not contributed to the ideological development of the disabled people's democratic movement for emancipation in this world, setting himself up as the ideological conscience of disabled people in non-Western rural areas. (Finkelstein, 29 November 1996, Internet 'Disability-research')

The emergence of rights as entitlement has influenced much of the discourse in relation to disability issues. This is closely linked to the emergence of Disability Studies as the examination of the social consequences of a disabling environment, rather than any exploration of individual biological inferiority. In the last ten years, not only has the recognition of the rights of women and black people become accepted, but discrimination on such grounds is deemed to be offensive to an educated mind. It is troublesome to see that for a number of reasons such equality is still not granted to disabled people. It leaves a number of questions to be addressed, e.g. are rights attributes to which we are all entitled or do they have to be earned? Are they entitlements to be received or must they be fought for? From the perspective of disabled people who are emerging as a recognised political movement, equality means the acceptance that disabled people are equal citizens and that social barriers, discrimination and prejudice which are associated with an impairment have to be removed:

> the main way to change structures is to enable disabled people to exercise agency – as direct action protestors, self-organised groups, lobbying groups etc. – which is only likely where disabled people have self-esteem,

pride etc. I have yet to see a research report which directly changed structures. (Shakespeare, 16 December 1996, Internet 'Disability-research')

Inclusion

The discussion about rights and entitlements has been linked to a range of
attempts to counter differences and inequality in society. Equality in its turn
assumes that similarly situated people are prepared to treat each other in a
similar fashion. However, it overlooks, or more particularly fails to indicate,
the element of responsibility that is anticipated as a consequence of rights. As
Gooding (1994) reminds us, this formal model of equality suggests that rights
are being perceived as achievements that are gained as a consequence of struggle and are an end in themselves, rather than a shared, collaborative part of
human endeavour to morally improve as a society. They can only operate in
the absence of any relevant differences between members of protected groups
and the rest of society. Any discourse around inclusion and the equality of
minority groups has to recognise that this issue of differences is fundamental.
The assertion of difference by dominant groups meant that early attempts
to counter discrimination tended to reinforce stereotypes (i.e. a white able-
bodied and essentially male 'norm'). Not only does this tend to perpetuate
superiority, manifested in a hierarchy of status, but it forces oppressed
groups to attempt to counteract, or even deny the presence of, differences in
the belief that to be 'normal' is to conform and to be assimilated.

French (1994) has suggested the pressure to be 'normal' in society is often
conducted at the expense of disabled people's needs and rights. Morris (1993)
also believes that the assumption that disabled people want to be normal,
rather than as they are, is one of the most oppressive experiences to which
disabled people are subjected. Morris rejects the view that it is progressive and
liberating to ignore differences. She maintains that disabled people have the
right to be both equal and different: 'I do not want to have to try to emulate
what a non-disabled woman looks like in order to assert positive things about
myself. I want to be able to celebrate my difference, not hide from it' (Morris
1991, p. 184).

Social acceptance is ever more tightly constrained in ideologies of 'getting
on'; succeeding in education and in market-led values of personal competitive-
ness. These expectations can lead many disabled people to try and become
superhuman, in order to avoid the negative connotations of helplessness and
personal incompetence. French (1994) gives the examples of deaf people who
learn to talk, blind people who are taught to use facial expressions appropri-
ately and people with Down's Syndrome having plastic surgery, as some of

the more doubtful opportunities offered to people with impairments. These interventions have been offered in the belief that they will help to overcome lack of social acceptability, reduce isolation and improve chances to compete with non-disabled people.

The emphasis on inclusion without sensitivity to its consequences may, however, lead non-disabled people to deny or fail to believe that a person's impairment or disability exists. There are a number of implications – one is the denial to the right to be disabled and to identify with and be proud of engaging in the struggle for the acceptance of disablement as a political identity. This is particularly the case with those who have relatively hidden impairments who manage to 'pass' as normal. This gives rise to the erroneous assumption that disabled people are just like everyone else. This is one of the messages that can be inferred from some of the more poorly considered first attempts at writing equal opportunities statements. The 'lack of acceptance by non-disabled people of the reality of disability, can lead disabled people to deny and minimise the oppression and difficulties they face' (French 1994a, p. 53).

The concept of autonomy and social justice

Whilst it is impossible to provide a complete and definitive explanation of social justice, the idea fits with any discussion of rights, fairness and choice in relation to policy and practices concerning the lives of disabled people. This book has indicated many examples of the ways in which people with disabilities, as a group, have been subject to treatment that is fundamentally unjust. Policy and practices in education, the medical service and employment all demonstrate examples of the discrimination that is still shown towards disabled people. It is nevertheless a feature of the changing nature of society that the fragmentation of group action as a method of realising change has been replaced by the demands for individual autonomy, choice and justice. Disabled people are beginning to operate with a collective voice and setting out to claim social justice as a rights issue. At the same time there are clear indications that there have been shifts in the perceptions and meaning of equal opportunities. Other interpretations of social justice are emerging. Equal opportunity is being redefined within a framework of individualism, entitlement and power rather than collective responsibility and the redistribution of wealth and reward. This places people who feel marginalised through economic circumstances and simple prejudice at a further disadvantage as the agenda of social justice is altered. The concept of social justice as a mutual consensus and cooperation in equal shares of any collective surplus managed by the state has changed to a perception of social justice as individual entitlement. This view, drawn primarily from right-wing political thinkers in the United States, is predicated on the belief that justice emerges from self-interest rather than collective endeavour and depends upon what individuals bring to a relationship or exchange for their mutual interest, rather than upon distributing any collective surplus that emerges from collective or group activity. Thus, social justice is an entitlement to exercise power, particularly by individuals rather than groups. Such free-market thinking suggests that the only basis for helping the less fortunate is through the voluntary transfer of goods and benefits from those who have more, to those who have less. This raises the question of whether a fair society is possible without the means of some control from an executive authority that determines the manner by which it is to be paid for. A society consisting solely of uncontrolled individuals raises spectres of at best charity handouts, benign neglect and a further marginalisation for groups considered to be economically redundant or 'unfit' (Mitthaug 1996).

Many of the early reformers who had advocated more humane treatment of people with disabilities had argued that disabled people should have access to the same rights and social resources as 'normal' people. This philosophy lies at the heart of Wolfensberger's (1983) construct of 'normalisation' and assumes that social justice resides in equality of access to treatment, welfare services and the physical environment.

Wolfensberger's view of justice is consistent with a theory of justice that focuses on individual rights rather than institutions. The contested term 'social justice' has been most eloquently examined by Rawls (1971) and is based on the tension between market- and state-oriented ideas of a fair and just distribution of social goods. Rawls argues that there are two basic principles in maintaining socially just practices. First that each person should 'have the most extensive basic liberty compatible with similar liberty for others'. Secondly he suggests that primary social goods should be distributed equally, with the exception of an unequal distribution which favoured those who are socially disadvantaged. The distributive view of social justice regards it as a responsibility of the state to provide for the needs of disabled people. As Christensen and Rizvi (1996) have pointed out, this perception of social justice as distributive efficiency influenced initial policy reforms of services for disabled people. For example, in relation to the education of students with disabilities social justice was perceived as fairer educational opportunities and based on the assessment of individual needs. Fairness of distribution was nevertheless still focussed around problematic and narrow assumptions of 'normal' individual behaviour, rather than a fundamental reappraisal of the ideologies, attitudes and assumptions inherent in society as a whole.

The notion that social injustice towards disabled people can be overcome by a distributive state welfare system that equates with social justice is clearly

insufficient in the current economic, political and cultural climate. The case
has been made succinctly:

> distributive solutions to social injustice fail to recognise power relation-
> ships which shape and sustain injustice. People with disabilities continue
> to be culturally oppressed and socially marginalised while their interests
> are still defined by advocates acting on their behalf. People with disabili-
> ties continue to demand the right to define what is in their best interests.
> (Christensen and Rizvi 1996, p. 4)

The analysis of what constitutes the 'best interests' of disabled people
seems to lie at the heart of the purpose and future of Disability Studies. Commentators who strongly identify themselves with the needs and rights of
disabled people advocate a radical policy of inclusion. They demand and define equality of opportunity in terms of location in the political process and,
in particular, critics of inclusion suggest that disabled people require services
to be managed on their behalf, as they will continue to face serious and
chronic barriers to achievements over their lifespan and will not be able to
compete successfully with non-disabled people.

Since the 1950s the costs of the welfare state in the United Kingdom have
risen with structural changes in employment patterns and shifts in the demo-
graphic trends of the population. People are living longer and the workforce
is declining. Changes in the labour market have seen a decline in manufacturing industry, an increase in part-time work and the 'feminisation of labour'
with the consequent growth in service industries, deregulation of working
practices and the demands for flexibility from employers. Long-term unemployment and changes from a passive welfare state to a more active and
judgemental benefits system has caused many people to become ineligible for
benefit payments. For example, in the United Kingdom, it is estimated that
the Jobseekers Allowance has eliminated many people from being visible on
the unemployment register (Finn 1997). This deliberate strategy of requiring
people to be active and earning their benefit, rather than remaining legitimate
but passive recipients of welfare, has affected the philosophy and response to
both unemployed people and other marginalised groups in society, including
those who are disabled.

Some warning shots

Legislation is in place that is designed to determine equality of opportunity
for disabled people. However, the outcome of any legislation depends on
what people do at local level and the relative newness of anti-discriminatory

legislation means that it is vulnerable to the 'watering down' effects of compromise as disabled people are expected 'to be reasonable' in the face of public expenditure cuts. A backlash against the costs of addressing disability issues has begun to be identified in the USA (Johnstone 1996c); the notion of the deserving and the undeserving is beginning to once more re-emerge and prompt moves to exclude some people with certain types of disabilities, e.g. those with HIV/AIDS.

The disability movement across the Western world is experiencing 'establishment backlash' and a 'greying of the leadership' as the original firebrands of the disability rights movement grow older or are sucked into the bureaucracy of mainstream provision of services and care. To some extent this illuminates the very success of the case for disability rights and legitimates the need for the study of disability as an academic discipline. At the same time it suggests that Disability Studies is, itself, vulnerable to attacks from more established forms of academic enquiry. When a backlash occurs against any cause, it emerges because the movement is perceived as a threat. In previous times, disabled people and the study of disability issues were viewed as merely a charity case deserving of sympathy. The disability movement is now demanding that disabled people be treated as equal citizens and disabled people are experiencing 'establishment backlash' such as the withdrawal of the preferential treatment associated with parking places for disabled people, the refusal to allow car use in pedestrianised town centres. It is the role of Disability Studies to evaluate and critically appraise such developments.

Disability Studies provides an opportunity to develop the analysis of a number of strands that have tended to remain separate. Psychological explanations of impairment or the interpretations of disability as individual loss need to be addressed, as do the social influences that tend to stigmatise disabled people. The voice of disabled people themselves has seldom been taken seriously. However, Disability Studies encourages disabled people to speak out and their inner voice to be listened to. Moreover, the discipline brings the two constituencies of disabled and non-disabled people together and allows people to speak of how disability issues affect their own lives.

The realisation that most disabled people are essentially non-political takes some time to dawn for many students of Disability Studies. However, perhaps this is not altogether surprising. Disabled people experience disability initially as a biological/medically determined and socially stigmatised impairment, without appreciating the political associations of disablement as a form of social, cultural and patriarchal oppression. It can be argued that the course of most people's lives is built around a tacit and unconscious acknowledgement of patriarchy and paternalism. For example, our personal agendas or day-to-day circumstances are essentially determined by the interests of parents, carers or the state. Thus, in these circumstances, it is easier to relinquish responsibility to others in the belief that, in general, they are setting out to 'do good'. The outcomes achieved are effectively theirs to control and resolve (e.g. all parents to a greater or lesser extent take on board some responsibility towards their own children). Most of us break away from these ties in our adolescence and early adulthood. For these very reasons, it takes an act of conscious will for a disabled person to remove themselves from this form of patriarchy, be it from a parent or the State.

Disability from this point of view is both deliberately created and perpetuated; it is part of the defining relationship between the impairment of an individual and the material environment within which the individual functions. It is socially created barriers that attach the precise meanings and boundaries of the disability for the individual with an impairment and it is the environmental context that defines the person as disabled. Moreover, it is the disabled person and their carers who then face the task of making sense of this relationship and, if motivated, who struggle to transform this construction. These struggles may take place in terms of either an individual or the actions of a group.

For disabled people, life circumstances appear to be determined far more significantly by issues that are beyond impairment. Physical dysfunction is a factor, but it is a constant. The less certain features of a lifestyle, such as income or day-to-day health, are perceived as separate and more pressing than the known, enduring considerations of physical loss or pain. In other words, for many people, and particularly those with low incomes, daily living is embedded in wider aspects of impoverishment and oppression. This aspect of disability research is not directly associated with the discrimination and exclusion experienced by disabled people. However, it emphasises how any two people may experience their impairments in different ways and construct differing identities for themselves, and this is important too for the future of Disability Studies. The personal experience of impairment is a critical element in the construction of personal identity and therefore disability research. But it does not negate the fact that people of difference may also be discriminated against collectively and that these acts of discrimination require exposure and explanation.

Changes in definition

The discussion of definition brings the debate around disability and Disability Studies back to some of the issues first raised in Chapter 1. During 1997 the World Health Organisation began debating the need to revise the

International Classification of Impairments, Disabilities and Handicaps (ICIDH) as originally promoted in 1980. The proposed new classification of conditions has undergone a significant revision and the title of the ICIDH has been changed from Impairment, Disabilities and Handicaps to ICIDH-2 International Classification of Impairments, Activities and Participation.

This new classification is undergoing systematic field trials and consultation, with a final version expected in 1999. The rationale for this change is 'to avoid the negative connotations of certain of the terms previously used' (World Health Organisation 1997, p. 1). The WHO has, thus, retained the descriptor 'impairment', but replaced the term 'disability' with what is considered a more neutral term, 'activity', and any negative associations in this dimension are described as 'activity limitations'. The term 'handicap' has been replaced by the alternative 'participation', and the negative associations in this dimension are described as 'participation restrictions'.

The original ICIDH classifications of impairment, disablement and handicap as functional difficulties were intended to call attention to the variations of difference within individual health conditions which may apply to everybody. However, inevitably the classification has tended to become a shorthand, associating an individual with a category of medical loss or disadvantage. In the 1980s the creation of the three dimensions was considered by some disabled people as a step forward in developing the recognition that society has the potential to be oppressive. However, as political awareness of disability has grown and the social model of disability has become better understood, the framework of the ICIDH has itself come to be considered oppressive. From its use as a classification at a level of individual need for treatment for specific conditions, it is now anticipated that ICIDH-2 will have relevance for broader areas of social policy. The compilers of the ICIDH-2 explicitly acknowledge that disablement is a process that operates at broadly two levels: the environmental and the personal. Environmental factors are considered extrinsic to, and outside the individual (these may include social attitudes, the legal system and architecture), while the personal factors may include fitness, health conditions, age, gender, psychological well-being and other characteristics. These personal factors differ from the environmental but have an impact on how disablement is experienced. At present no personal factors are listed in the classification and their assessment is left to the discretion of the users.

This revision of the WHO classification recommends that the term 'disability' be dropped. This has a number of implications for both disabled people and the shaping of attitudes in society towards disablement. It is difficult to believe that those who have developed a political awareness and pride in the status of being a 'disabled person' will be altered by these changes; but there is the potential to confuse both the construction and the experience of disability, conflating them with particular individual health conditions and personal experiences. The ICIDH-2 classification continues to emphasise what people can't do, rather than celebrating what they can, arising from a health condition. The classification, thereby, continues to undermine the collective voice of disabled people in their attempts to seek out an alternative terminology of their own choosing.

It is also evident from the WHO deliberations on classifications that the European perspective on disablement, which emphasises the imposition of a disability on a person by society, is at odds with that applying in North America and Australia, where disablement is associated more with an acquired pathology or condition. This suggests that the political consciousness of disabled people in Europe is, at present, more assertive than elsewhere in the world. (The full draft version of ICIDH-2 is available on the Internet at the following address: http://www.who.ch/icidh.)

Summary

Social justice and its political consequences is a particular concern for the study of disability issues in the UK. Nevertheless, most disabled people are not politically active and their experience of disability is initially a consequence of accident or a biologically/medically determined and socially stigmatising health condition. The political associations of disablement as a form of social, cultural and patriarchal oppression only emerge slowly. The chapter argues that the course of most people's lives is built around a tacit and unconscious acknowledgement of patriarchy and paternalism and that in these circumstances it is easier to relinquish responsibility to others in the belief that, in general, they are setting out to 'do good'. Finally, the chapter briefly explores some of the strengths and weaknesses in the proposed changes in the WHO classifications of impairment, disability and handicaps.

Conclusion

For students of Disability Studies, especially in a post-modern era that is seeking to redefine the direction of social movements, it is important to remember that the life circumstances of disabled people are determined far more significantly by issues that are beyond physical loss or impairment. The less certain features of a lifestyle, such as income or day-to-day health, are perceived as separate and sometimes more pressing than the known, enduring considerations of physical loss or pain.

That disablement is a socially constructed concept in the service and shaping of power is now a generally accepted orthodoxy. Disability Studies is beginning to develop its own critical terminology to address these concerns and offers an epistemology that can run counter to standard scientific practices and explanations. As an emerging discipline it not only promises the opportunity for emancipation through critique and research, but also suggests new insights and frameworks for understanding human behaviour and interaction. Nevertheless, like all new areas of scholarship, Disability Studies must beware of generating its own set of stereotypical assumptions (e.g. that the social model of disablement offers a sufficient explanation of causation). In similar fashion, students setting out on a programme of Disability Studies must not become too defensive, or apologetic, when challenged in their attempts to establish the social critique of disablement as a legitimate area of academic discourse. Whilst academic analysis does not immediately help to explain to the individual with a severed spinal column how they can regain bladder and bowel control, it does something that is ultimately more important. It brings understanding through a variety of interpretations and links the circumstances of disablement to the totality of human experience. This allows a point of entry via one of the most powerful, but often disregarded, areas of all our academic lives: the imagination. Disability Studies helps students to connect scholarship with imagination and links the abstract claims of sociology and medical science with the concrete realities of people's lived experiences. Students of Disability Studies are setting out on an investigation that touches the boundaries of human dignity. As such, they confront rather than hide from the collective responsibility that we have towards each other.

References

Allen, A. (1997) 'Policing the gene machine: can anyone control the human genome project?', *Lingua Franca* **7**(3), 28–37.

Bach, M. and Rioux, M. (1996) 'Social well-being: a framework for quality of life research', in Renwick, R., Brown, I., Nagler, M. (eds) *Quality of Life in Health Promotion and Rehabilitation*. London: Sage.

Baine, D. (1988) *Handicapped Children in Developing Countries*. Edmonton: University of Alberta.

Banfelvy, C. (1996) 'The paradox of the quality of life of adults with learning difficulties', *Disability and Society* **11**(4), 569–78.

Barker, D. (1983) 'How to curb the fertility of the unfit: the feeble-minded in Edwardian Britain', *Oxford Review of Education* **9**(3), 197–211.

Barnes, C. (1990) *Cabbage Syndrome*. London: Falmer.

Barnes, C. (1994) *Disabled People in Britain and Discrimination*. London: Hurst and Co.

Barnes, C. (1996) 'Disability and the myth of the independent researcher', *Disability and Society* **11**(1), 107–10.

Barnes, C. and Mercer, G. (eds) (1996) *Exploring the Divide: Illness and Disability*. Leeds: The Disability Press.

Bauby, J.-D. (1997) *The Diving Bell and the Butterfly*. London: Fourth Estate.

Beardshaw, V. (1988) *Last on the List: Community Services for People with Physical Disabilities*. London: King's Fund.

Beck, U. (1995) *Ecological Politics in an Age of Risk*. Cambridge: Polity Press.

Bell, A. and Bhate, M. (1992) 'Prevalence of overweight and obesity in Down's Syndrome and other mentally handicapped adults living in the community', *Journal of Intellectual Disability Research* **36**, 359–64.

Benedict, R. (1934) *Patterns of Culture*. Boston: Houghton-Mifflin.

Beresford, P. and Harding, T. (eds) (1993) *A Challenge to Change: Practical Experiences of Building User-Led Services*. London: National Institute for Social Work.

Berrington, E. and Johnstone, D. (1994) *Disability and Health: The Concerns of Disabled People in West Lancashire*. Ormskirk: Edge Hill University College/West Lancashire Association of Disabled People.

Berrington, E., Cartwright, L., Johnstone, D. (1996) *The Life of the People*. Ormskirk: Edge Hill University College/West Lancashire Association of Disabled People.

Blanch, D. (1994) 'Employment integration, economic opportunity and the Americans with Disabilities Act: empirical study from 1990–1993', *Iowa Law Review* **79**(4), 854–923.

Booth, T. (1992) *Making Connections*. Milton Keynes: Open University Press.

Booth, T. (1996) 'Sounds of still voices: issues in the use of narrative methods with people who have learning difficulties', in Barton, L. (ed.) *Disability and Society: Emerging Issues and Insights*. London: Longman.

Borsay, A. (1986) 'Personal trouble or public issue? Towards a model of policy for people with physical and mental disabilities', *Disability, Handicap and Society* **1**(2).

Bottomore, T. and Marshall, T. H. (1992) *Citizenship and Social Class*. London: Pluto.

Bracking, S. (1993) 'An introduction to the idea of independent integrated living', in Barnes, C. (ed.) *Making our Own Choices: Independent Living, Personal Assistance and Disabled People*. London: BCODP.

Brisenden, S. (1986) 'Independent living and the medical model of disability', *Disability, Handicap and Society* 1(2), 173-8.

British Council of Disabled People (1994) *Access Denied: Human Rights and Disabled People*. London: Liberty.

Brown, R., Bayer, M., Brown, P. (1992) *Choices and Quality of Life*. London: Chapman and Hall.

Burke, E. (1995) *The Americans with Disabilities Act: Ensuring Equal Access to the American Dream*. Washington: National Council on Disability.

Burt C. (1925) *The Young Delinquent*. London: University of London Press.

Burt, C. (1938) *The Backward Child*. London: University of London Press.

Bury, M. (1996a) 'Defining and researching disability: challenges and responses', in Barnes, C. and Mercer, G. (eds) *Exploring the Divide: Illness and Disability*. Leeds: The Disability Press.

Bury, M. (1996b) 'Disability and the myth of the independent researcher: a reply', *Disability and Society* 11(1), 111–13.

Bynoe, I., Oliver, M., Barnes, C. (1991) *Equal Rights for Disabled People*. London: Institute of Public Policy Research.

Campbell, J. and Oliver, M. (1996) *Disability Politics: Understanding our Past, Changing our Future*. London: Routledge.

Cartwright, L., Berrington, E., Johnstone, D. (1996) *The Voice of the People*. Ormskirk: Edge Hill University College/West Lancashire Association of Disabled People.

Central Statistical Office (1996) *Social Trends*. London: CSO.

Chapman, T., Johnstone, D., Roberts, K., Wilson, R. (1997) *Measurements of 'Quality of Life' and Services for People with Learning Difficulties and their Carers in the North West of England*. Ormskirk: Edge Hill University College.

Child Poverty Action Group (1994a) *Rights Guide to Non-means-tested Benefits*, 17th edn. London: CPAG.

Child Poverty Action Group (1994b) *National Welfare Benefits Handbook*, 24th edn. London: CPAG.

Christensen, C. and Rizvi, F. (1996) *Disability and the Dilemmas of Education and Justice*. Buckingham: Open University Press.

Coleridge, P. (1993) *Disability, Liberation and Development*. Oxford: Oxfam.

Cooper, D. (1996) 'Gathering evidence in the USA', *Skill Journal* 55, 24-8.

Corbett, J. (1996) *Badmouthing: The Language of Special Needs*. London: Falmer Press.

Corbett, J. and Barton, L. (1992) *The Struggle for Choice*. London: Routledge.

Craft, A. (1992) *Aspects of Adulthood: Sex Education in Further Education for Learners with Severe Learning Difficulties*. London: FEU.

Crawley, B. (1988) *The Growing Voice: A Survey of Self-advocacy Groups in Adult Training Centres and Hospitals in Great Britain*. London: CMH.

Crawley, B. (1989) *Independent Living for Adults with Mental Handicap*. London: Cassell.

Crow, L. (1996) 'Including all our lives: renewing the social model of disability', in Barnes, C. and Mercer, G. (eds) *Exploring the Divide: Illness and Disability*. Leeds: The Disability Press.

Darnborough, A. and Kinrade, D. (eds) (1996) *Directory for Disabled People*. London: Woodhead-Faulkner.

Daunt, P. (1991) *Meeting Disability: A European Response*. London: Cassell.

de Crespigny, L. with Dredge, R. (1991) *Which Tests for my Unborn Baby?* Melbourne, Australia: Oxford University Press.

DfEE (1994) *Code of Practice: On the Identification and Assessment of Special Educational Needs*. London: HMSO.

DHSS (1988) *Caring for People* (The Griffiths Report). London: HMSO.

Disabled People's International (1982) *Proceedings of the First World Congress*. Singapore: DPI.

Disability Awareness in Action (1993) *Disability Awareness in Action: Consultation and Influence*. London: Disability Awareness in Action.

Disability Now (1996) *The Disability Manifesto: What Has to be Done*. London: Scope/Creative Press.

Driedger, D. (1989) *The Last Civil Rights Movement*. London: Hurst.

Dugdale, R. (1877) *The Jukes, A Study in Crime, Pauperism, Disease and Heredity*. New York: New York Prison Association, 31st Annual Report.

Edinburgh Review (1865) 'Idiot asylums', *Edinburgh Review* **122**, 37–72.

Ephraem, L. (1984) *Health of One Million*. New York: UNICEF.

Erlanger, H. and Roth, W. (1985) 'Disability policy: the parts and the whole', *American Behavioural Scientist* **28**(3).

Fagan, T. and Lee, P. (1997) 'New social movements and social policy: a case study for the disability movement', in Lavalette, M. and Pratt, A. (eds) *Social Policy: A Conceptual and Theoretical Introduction*. London: Sage.

Felce, D. and Perry, J. (1996) 'Exploring current conceptions of quality of life', in Renwick, R., Brown, I., Nagler, M. (eds) *Quality of Life in Health Promotion and Rehabilitation*. London: Sage.

Finch, J. and Groves, D. (1983) *A Labour of Love: Women, Work and Caring*. London: Routledge and Kegan Paul.

Finkelstein, V. (1979) *Attitudes and Disabled People: Issues for Discussion*. New York: World Rehabilitation Fund.

Finkelstein, V. (1993) 'Disability – a social challenge or an administrative responsibility?', in Swain, J., Finkelstein, V., French, S., Oliver, M. (eds) *Disabling Barriers – Enabling Environments*. London: Sage/Open University.

Finkelstein, V. and French, S. (1993) 'Towards a psychology of disability', in Swain, J., Finkelstein, V., French, S., Oliver, M. (eds). *Disabling Barriers – Enabling Environments*. London: Sage/Open University.

Finn, D. (1997) Jobseeker's Allowance Conference, 14 March, University of Portsmouth.

Flynn, M. (1989) *Independent Living for Adults with Mental Handicap*. London: Cassell.

Flynn, M. and Hirst, M. (1992) *This Year, Next Year, Sometime . . . ? Learning Disability and Adulthood*. London: National Development Team/Social Policy Research Unit.

Fong, C. and Brodeur, G. (1987) 'Down's Syndrome and leukemia: epidemiology, genetics, cytogenetics and mechanisms of leukemogenesis, *Cancer, Genetics and Cytogenetics* **28**, 55–76.

Food Magazine (1997) 'Food supplements – has the hype gone too far?' **38**, August, p. 1.

Fox, R. Haniotes, H., Rotatori, A. (1984) 'A streamlined weight loss program for moderately retarded adults in a sheltered workshop setting', *Applied Research in Mental Retardation* **5**, 69–79.

Freeman, A. (1988) 'Who's moving the goal posts?', in Barton, L. (ed.) *The Politics of Special Educational Needs*. London: Falmer Press.

French, S. (ed.) (1992) *Physiotherapy: A Psychosocial Approach*. Oxford: Butterworth-Heinemann.

French, S. (1993) 'Disability, impairment or something in between?', in Swain, J., Finkelstein, V., French, S., Oliver, M. (eds) *Disabling Barriers – Enabling Environments*. London: Sage/OU.

French, S. (1994a) 'Researching disability', in French, S. (ed.) *On Equal Terms: Working with Disabled People*. Oxford: Butterworth-Heinemann.

French, S. (1994b) 'Ageism', in French, S. (ed.) *Physiotherapy: A Psychosocial Approach*, 2nd edn. Oxford: Butterworth-Heinemann.

Garrow, J. (1988) *Obesity and Related Diseases*. Edinburgh: Churchill-Livingstone.

Gillespie-Sells, K. and Campbell, J. (1991) *Disability Equality Training Trainers Guide*. London: Central Council for Education and Training in Social Work.

Gillott, J. (1997) 'Gene junction', *Guardian*, 20 February 1997, p. 14.

Goddard, H. (1912) *The Kallikak Family*. New York: Macmillan.

Goffman, F. (1970) *Stigma: Notes on the Management of Spoiled Identity*. London: Penguin.

Gooding, C. (1994) *Disabling Laws, Enabling Acts*. London: Pluto.

Gould, S. J. (1996) *The Mismeasure of Man*, rev. edn. London: Penguin.

Griffiths, M. (1990) 'Enabled to work', in Griffiths, M. *Working Together*. London: FEU.

Griffiths, R. (1988) *Community Care: Agenda for Action*. London: HMSO.

Guardian (1997a) 'Scientist scorn sci-fi fears over sheep clone', 24 February 1997, 7.

Guardian (1997b) 'Scientists "able to create human clone"', 26 February 1997, 6.

Haffter, C. (1968) 'The changeling: history and psychodynamics of attitudes to handicapped children in European folk-lore', *Journal of History of Behavioural Sciences* 4, 55–61.

Hameister, H. (1996) 'The human genome project in progress: the construction and meaning of the genetic map', in Wilczek, I. (ed.) *Biomedical Research and Patenting: Ethical Social and Legal Aspects.* Baarn: European Platform for Patients' Organisations.

Harbert, W. (1988) 'Dignity and choice', *Insight*, 25 March.

Hariharan, S. (1982) 'CBR Manual in practice', *One in Ten* 2(2), 2.

Hawkridge, D. and Vincent, T. (1992) *Learning Difficulties and Computers: Access to the Curriculum.* London: Jessica Kingsley.

Hegarty, S. (1993) *Meeting Special Needs in Ordinary Schools.* London: Cassell.

Heise, L. (1992) *Violence, Health and Development Project.* New Brunswick, NJ: Women's Global Leadership, Rutgers University.

Helander, B. (1988) *Family Health Management in the Gansaxdheere District of the Bay Region, Somalia.* Mogadishu, Somalia: UNICEF.

Helander, E., Mendis, P., Nelson, G. (1983) *Training Disabled People in the Community*, 3rd edn. Geneva: World Health Organisation.

Helander, E. (1993) *Prejudice and Dignity: An Introduction to Community Based Rehabilitation.* New York: UNDP.

Henwood, M. (1990) 'No sense of urgency: age discrimination in health care', in McEwen, E. (ed.) *Age: The Unrecognised Discrimination*, 43–57. London: Age Concern.

Herrnstein, R., and Murray, C. (1994) *The Bell Curve: The Re-shaping of American Life by Difference in Intelligence.* New York: Free Press.

Hevey, D. (1992) *The Creatures Time Forgot.* London: Routledge.

Hirst, J. (1996) 'People power', *Community Care* 1141, October, 23.

HMSO (1992) *The Health of the Nation*, Cm 1986. London: HMSO.

HMSO (1995) *The Health of the Nation: A Strategy for People with Learning Disabilities.* London: Department of Health.

HMSO (1996) *Disability Discrimination Act 1995.* London: HMSO.

Howells, G. (1989) 'Down's Syndrome and the general practitioner', *Journal of the Royal College of General Practitioners* 39, 470–75.

Hughes, A., McAuslane, L., Schur, H. (1996) 'Comparing quality of life for people with learning disabilities and people who are unemployed or retired', *British Journal of Learning Disabilities* 24, 99–104.

Hugill, B. (1997) 'Britain's expansion zone', *The Observer*, 13 April, 29.

Huitt, K. and Elston, R. (1991) 'Attitudes towards persons with disabilities expressed by professional counsellors', *Journal of Applied Rehabilitation Counselling*, 22(2), 42–3.

Imrie, R. (1996) *Disability and the City: International Perspectives.* London: Paul Chapman.

Ingstad, B. and Reynolds-Whyte, S. (eds) (1995) *Disability and Culture.* Berkeley: University of California.

Jancar, J. (1990) 'Cancer and mental handicap: a further study', *British Journal of Psychiatry* 156, 531–3.

Jensen, E. (1995) *Super Teaching.* Delmar, Calif.: Turning Point.

Jewson, N. and Mason, D. (1986) 'The theory and practice of equal opportunities: liberal and radical approaches', *Sociological Review* 34(2).

Johnstone, D. (1995) *Further Opportunities: Learning Difficulties and Disabilities in Further Education.* London: Cassell.

Johnstone, D. (1996a) 'Inclusive education and community: integrating the special professional'. Paper given to the European Forum, Lucenec, 13–18 May.

Johnstone, D. (1996b) 'Transition to further education for students with learning difficulties and disabilities', *Innovation in Learning in Education: The International Journal for the Reflective Practitioner* 2(3), 11–17.

Johnstone, D. (1996c) 'The decline of disability leadership in California'. Unpublished paper, Edge Hill University College.

Kalyanpur, M. (1996) 'The influence of Western special education on community-based services in India', *Disability and Society* 11(2), 249–66.

Kennedy, H. (Chair) (1997) *Learning Works*. Coventry: FEFC.

Kennedy, I. (1980) 'Reith Lectures', London: British Broadcasting Corporation (also *The Listener)*.

Kent, A. (1996) 'Patients' views of patenting', in Wilczek, I. (ed.) *Biomedical Research and Patenting: Ethical Social and Legal Aspects*. Baarn: European Platform for Patients' Organisations.

Kurtz, R. (1964) 'Implications of recent sociological research in mental retardation', *American Journal of Mental Deficiency* **69**, 506–10.

Levine, D. (1985) *The Flight from Ambiguity: Essays in Social and Cultural Theory*. Chicago: University of Chicago Press.

Liggett, H. (1988) 'Stars are not born: an interactive approach to the politics of disability', *Disability, Handicap and Society* **3**(3), 6–13.

Loney, M. (1983) 'The politics of self help and community care', in Brechin, A. *et al.* (eds) *Handicap in a Social World*. London: Hodder & Stoughton.

Lyons, M. and Hayes, R. (1993) 'Student perceptions of persons with psychiatric and other disorders', *The American Journal of Occupational Therapy* **47**(6), 541–8.

Malson, L. and Itard, J. (1972) *Wolf Children and The Wild Boy of Aveyron*. London: NLB.

Marris, V. (1996) *Lives Worth Living*. London: Pandora Books.

Marshall, G. (1976) *The Challenge of a Handicap*. Coventry: Exhall Grange.

Martin, J., Meltzer, H., Elliot, D. (1988) *The Prevalence of Disability among Adults*. London: HMSO.

McEwen, E. (ed.) (1990) *Age: The Unrecognised Discrimination*. London: Age Concern.

McKnight, J. (1995) *The Careless Society: Community and its Counterfeits*. New York: Basic Books.

Miles, M. (1981) *Handicapped Children and their Needs in the North West Frontier Province of Pakistan*. Peshawar: Mental Health Centre.

Miles, M. (1985) *Where there is no Rehabilitation Plan: A Critique of the who Scheme and Suggestions for Future Direction*. Peshawar: Mental Health Centre.

Miles, M. (1990) 'The "community base" in rehabilitation planning: key or gimmick?', in Thorburn, M. and Marfo, K. (eds.) *Practical Approaches to Childhood Disability in Developing Countries: Insights from Experience and Research*. St. John's: University of Newfoundland.

Miles, M. (1995) 'Disability in an eastern religious context: historical perspectives', *Disability and Society* **10**(1), 49–70.

Miles, S. (1996) 'Engaging with the disability rights movement,: the experience of community-based rehabilitation in Southern Africa', *Disability and Society* **11**(4), 501–17.

Mitthaug, D. (1996) *Equal Opportunity Theory*. London: Sage.

Moniga, S. and Vianello, R. (1995) *Job Possibilities and Quality of Life for Handicapped People in Europe*. Karlsruhe: European Association for Special Education.

Morris, J. (1991) *Pride Against Prejudice*. London: The Women's Press.

Morris, J. (1993) *Independent Lives: Community Care and Disabled People*. Basingstoke: Macmillan.

Morris, J. (ed.) (1996) *Encounters with Strangers: Feminism and Disability*. London: The Women's Press.

Morris, J. and Winn, H. (1993) *Housing and Social Inequality*. London: Hilary Shipman.

Morrissey, P. (1991) *A Primer for Corporate America on Civil Rights for the Disabled*. Horsham, Penn.: LRP Publications.

Moss, S. (1995) 'Methodological issues in the diagnosis of psychiatric disorders in adults with learning disability', *Thornfield Journal* (University of Dublin).

Napolitano, S. (1996) 'Mobility impairment, in Hales, G. (ed.) *Beyond Disability: Towards an Enabling Society*. London: Sage.

National Heart Forum (1997) *The Price of Poverty*. London: The National Heart Forum.

Nimbkar, E. (1971) 'Simple aids for handicapped children in India', *International Rehabilitation Review* **22**, 6–8.

Nirje, B. (1980) 'The normalisation principle', in Flynn, R. and Nitsch, K. (eds) *Normalization, Social Integration and Community Services*. Baltimore: University Park Press.

Nkabinde, Z. (1993) 'The role of special education in a changing South Africa', *The Journal of Special Education* **27**(1), 107–14.

O'Brien, J. and Tyne, A. (1981) *The Principles of Normalisation: A Foundation for Effective Services*. London: The Campaign for Mentally Handicapped People.

O'Brien, K., Tate, K., Zaharia, E. (1991) 'Mortality in a large southeastern facility for persons with mental retardation', *American Journal of Mental Retardation* **95**, 397–403.

O'Day, B. (1996) 'Re-authorization of the rehabilitation act: comprehensive solutions or political satisficing?', *Disability and Society* **11**(3), 411–27.

O'Toole, B. (1987) 'Community based rehabilitation: problems and possibilities', *European Journal of Special Needs Education* **2**(3), 177–90.

Office of Health Economics (1990) *Osteoporosis and the Risk of Fractures*. London: OHE.

Oliver, M. (1983) *Social Work with Disabled People*. Basingstoke: Macmillan.

Oliver, M. (1990) *The Politics of Disablement*. Basingstoke: Macmillan.

Oliver, M. (1992) 'Changing the social relations of research production', *Disability, Handicap and Society* **7**(2), 101–14.

Oliver, M. (1996a) *Understanding Disability: From Theory to Practice*. Basingstoke: Macmillan.

Oliver, M. (1996b) 'Defining impairment and disability: issues at stake', in Barnes, C. and Mercer, G. (eds) *Exploring the Divide: Illness and Disability*. University of Leeds: Disability Press.

Oliver, M. and Zarb, G. (1989) 'The politics of disability: a new approach', *Disability, Handicap and Society* **14**(3), 221–40.

Pfieffer, D. (1996) '"We won't go back": the ADA on the grassroots level', *Disability and Society* **11**(2), 271–83.

Quereshi, H. and Nocon, A. (1996) *Report on Expert Seminars on Routine Outcome Measurement in Personal Social Services*. DH 1378, 29 February 1996. York: SPRU.

Rawls, J. (1971) *A Theory of Justice*. Cambridge, Mass.: Belknap.

Ray, L. (1983) 'Eugenics, mental deficiency and Fabian socialism between the wars', *Oxford Review of Education* **9**(3), 213–25.

Renwick, R. and Friefeld, S. (1996) 'Quality of life and rehabilitation', in Renwick, R., Brown, I., Nagler, M. (eds) *Quality of Life in Health Promotion and Rehabilitation*. London: Sage.

Rioux, M. (1996) 'Overcoming the social construction of inequality as a prerequisite to quality of life', in Renwick, R., Brown, I., Nagler, M. (eds) *Quality of Life in Health Promotion and Rehabilitation*. London: Sage.

Rock, P. (1996) 'Eugenics and euthenasia: a cause for concern for disabled people, particularly disabled women', *Disability and Society* **11**(1), 121–7.

Rose, H. (1994) *Love, Power and Knowledge*. Cambridge: Polity Press.

Rosenqvist, J. (1993) 'The concept of integration in schools and society in connection with adult quality of life', in Moniga, S. and Vianello, R. (eds) *Job Possibilities and Quality of Life for Handicapped People in Europe*. Karlsruhe: European Association for Special Education.

Scholl, T., Stein, Z., Hansen, H. (1982) 'Leukaemia and other cancers, anomalies and infections as causes of death in Down's Syndrome in the United States during 1976', *Developmental Medicine and Child Neurology* **24**, 817–29.

Scope (1994) *Disabled in Britain*. London: Scope. (Published in three parts: *A World Apart* (lives of disabled people), *Behind Closed Doors* (parents and carers), *Counting on Community Care* (people's experiences of Health and Social Services).)

Shakespeare, T. (1993) 'Disabled people's self organisation: a new social movement?', *Disability, Handicap and Society* **8**(3), 249–64.

Shakespeare, T. (1995) 'Back to the future? New genetics and disabled people', *Critical Social Policy* **15**, Autumn, 22–35.

Shakespeare, T. (1996) 'Rules of engagement: doing disability research', *Disability and Society* **11**(1), March, 115–19.

Shakespeare, T. (1997) 'Reviewing the past, developing the future', *Skill Journal* **58**, 8–11.

Shakespeare, T., Gillespie-Sells, K., Davies, D. (1996) *The Sexual Politics of Disability*. London: Cassell.

Shakespeare, T. and Watson, N. (1997) 'Defending the social model', *Disability and Society* **12**(2), 293–300.

Silburn, L. (1993) 'A social model in a medical world: the development of the integrated living team as part of the strategy for younger physically disabled people in North Derbyshire', in Swain, J. *et al.* (eds) *Disabling Barriers: Enabling Environments*. London: Sage.

Snowdon, Lord (Chair) (1979) *Integrating the Disabled* (The Snowdon Report). Horsham: National

Fund for Research into Crippling Diseases.

Soder, M. (1980) 'School integration of the mentally retarded – analysis of concepts, research and research needs', in *Research and Development Concerning the Integration of Handicapped Pupils in the Ordinary School System*. Stockholm: Skoloverstyrelsen.

Steiner, R. (1994) *How to Know Higher Worlds*. New York: Anthroposophic Press.

Szivos, S. (1992) 'The limits of integration', in Brown, H. and Smith, H. (eds) *Normalisation: A Reader for the 90s*. London: Routledge.

Taylor, D. (1989) 'Citizenship and social power', *Critical Social Policy* **26**, 19.

Thomas, D. (1978) *The Social Psychology of Childhood Disability*. London: Methuen.

Thorburn, M. and Marfo, K. (1990) 'Practical approaches to childhood disability in developing countries', in Thorburn, M. and Marfo, K. (eds) *Insights from Experience and Research*. St. John's: University of Newfoundland.

Tomasky, M. (1996) 'Reaffirming our actions', *The Nation* **262**(19), 21–4.

Turk, V. and Brown, H. (1993) 'The sexual abuse of adults with learning disabilities: results of a two year survey', *Mental Handicap Research* **6**, 193–216.

Turner, S. (1996) 'Promoting healthy lifestyles for people with learning disabilities: a survey of provider organisations', *British Journal of Learning Disabilities* **24**, 138–44.

Turner, S. and Moss, S. (1995) *The Health Needs of Adults with Learning Disabilities and the Health of the Nation Strategy*. Manchester: Hester Adrian Research Centre.

Union of the Physically Impaired Against Segregation (1976) *Fundamental Principles of Disability*. London: UPIAS.

Vincent, T. (ed.) (1990) *New Technology, Disability and Special Educational Needs: Some Case Studies in Further Education*. Coventry: Hereward College.

Vincent, T. (1993) 'Foreword', in Broadbent, S. and Curran, S. (eds) *The Assessment, Disability and Technology Handbook*. Oldham: North West Access Centre.

Warnock, M. (Chair) (1978) *Special Educational Needs: Report of the Committee of Enquiry into the Education of Handicapped Children and Young People* (The Warnock Report). London: HMSO.

Warwick, C., Johnstone, D., Rodrigues, D., Janssen, M. (eds) (1997) *The Role of Resource Centres in Supporting Integration in Education*. Brussels: HELIOS Group 8.

Werner, D. (1987) *Disabled Village Children*. Palo Alto, Calif.: Hesperian Foundation.

Whelan, E. and Speake, B. (1977) *Adult Training Centres in England and Wales*. Manchester: University of Manchester Press.

Wilson, E. (1985) *Adorned in Dreams: Fashion and Modernity*. London: Virago Press.

Wilson, G. (ed.) (1996) *Community Care: Asking the Users*. London: Chapman and Hall.

Wiseman, J. (1978) 'The research web', in Bynner, J. and Stribley, K. (eds) *Social Research Principles and Procedures*. London: Longman.

Wolfenberger, W. (1983) 'Social role valorisation: a proposed new term for the principles of normalisation', *Mental Retardation* **19**(1), 1–7.

Wolff, H. (1980) 'Tools for living: a blue print for a major new industry', in Brechin, A. *et al.* (eds) *Handicap in a Social World*. London: Hodder & Stoughton.

Wood, P. (1980) *International Classification of Impairments, Disabilities and Handicaps*. Geneva: World Health Organisation.

World Health Organisation (1976) International Classification Document, A29/INF.DOC/1.

World Health Organisation (1982) *Community Based Rehabilitation. Report of a WHO interregional consultation*, 28 June–3 July, RHB/IR/82.1. Geneva: WHO.

Wright, T. and Leung, P. (1993) *Meeting the Unique Needs of Minorities with Disabilities*. Washington DC: National Council on Disability.

Zarb, G. (1993a) 'Ageing with a disability', in Johnson, J. and Slater, S. (eds) *Ageing and Later Life*. London: Sage.

Zarb, G. (1993b) 'The dual experience of ageing with a disability', in Swain, J. *et al.* (eds) *Disabling Barriers: Enabling Environments*. London: Sage.

Index